CCNA Exam

400 Questions for Guaranteed Success

Exam Code: 200-301

1st Edition

www.versatileread.com

Document Control

Proposal Name	:	CCNA Exam: 400 Questions for Guaranteed Success
Document Edition	:	1st
Document Release Date	:	25th July 2024
Reference	:	200-301
VR Product Code	:	20242602CCNA

About the Contributors:

Nouman Ahmed Khan

AWS/Azure/GCP-Architect, CCDE, CCIEx5 (R&S, SP, Security, DC, Wireless), CISSP, CISA, CISM, CRISC, ISO27K-LA is a Solution Architect working with a global telecommunication provider. He works with enterprises, mega-projects, and service providers to help them select the best-fit technology solutions. He also works as a consultant to understand customer business processes and helps select an appropriate technology strategy to support business goals. He has more than eighteen years of experience working with global clients. One of his notable experiences was his tenure with a large managed security services provider, where he was responsible for managing the complete MSSP product portfolio. With his extensive knowledge and expertise in various areas of technology, including cloud computing, network infrastructure, security, and risk management, Nouman has become a trusted advisor for his clients.

Abubakar Saeed

Abubakar Saeed is a trailblazer in the realm of technology and innovation. With a rich professional journey spanning over twenty-nine years, Abubakar has seamlessly blended his expertise in engineering with his passion for transformative leadership. Starting humbly at the grassroots level, he has significantly contributed to pioneering the Internet in Pakistan and beyond. Abubakar's multifaceted experience encompasses managing, consulting, designing, and implementing projects, showcasing his versatility as a leader.

His exceptional skills shine in leading businesses, where he champions innovation and transformation. Abubakar stands as a testament to the power of visionary leadership, heading operations, solutions design, and integration. His emphasis on adhering to project timelines and exceeding customer expectations has set him apart as a great leader. With an unwavering commitment to adopting technology for operational simplicity and enhanced efficiency, Abubakar Saeed continues to inspire and drive change in the industry.

Dr. Fahad Abdali

Dr. Fahad Abdali is an esteemed leader with an outstanding twenty-year track record in managing diverse businesses. With a stellar educational background, including a bachelor's degree from the prestigious NED University of Engineers & Technology and a Ph.D. from the University of Karachi, Dr. Abdali epitomizes academic excellence and continuous professional growth.

Dr. Abdali's leadership journey is marked by his unwavering commitment to innovation and his astute understanding of industry dynamics. His ability to navigate intricate challenges has driven growth and nurtured organizational triumph. Driven by a passion for excellence, he stands as a beacon of inspiration within the business realm. With his remarkable leadership skills, Dr. Fahad Abdali continues to steer businesses toward unprecedented success, making him a true embodiment of a great leader.

Muniza Kamran

Muniza Kamran is a technical content developer in a professional field. She crafts clear and informative content that simplifies complex technical concepts for diverse audiences, with a passion for technology. Her expertise lies in Microsoft, cybersecurity, cloud security, and emerging technologies, making her a valuable asset in the tech industry. Her dedication to quality and accuracy ensures that her writing empowers readers with valuable insights and knowledge. She has done certification in SQL database, database design, cloud solution architecture, and NDG Linux unhatched from CISCO.

Table of Contents

About CCNA Exam

Introduction

The Cisco Certified Network Associate (CCNA) course provides foundational information for all IT vocations. You will learn how to build, operate, configure, and verify basic IPv4 and IPv6 networks using a combination of workbooks, hands-on labs, and self-study. This course covers configuring network components such as switches, routers, and wireless LAN controllers, controlling network devices, and identifying fundamental security concerns. You will also learn about network programmability, automation, and software-defined networking.

The Cisco CCNA Certification is one of the most well-known network certifications in the industry. Almost one of every two network engineers has this Cisco certification. Whether or not they are studying for a networking certification, every network engineer is familiar with the CCNA (Cisco Certified Network Associate) certification.

CCNA 200-301 Certification is not only a vendor certification but also an industry standard demonstrating Networking Fundamentals knowledge.

Networking

Computer Networking conveys and exchanges data between nodes over a shared medium in an information system. Computer networking connects devices and endpoints on a Local Area Network (LAN), internet or a private Wide Area Network (WAN). This is a necessary function for service providers, businesses, and consumers worldwide to share resources, use or provide services, and communicate. Networking makes everything from phone calls to text messaging to streaming video to the Internet of Things (IoT) easier.

Networking combines a network's design and construction. It includes operating, managing, and maintaining the network infrastructure, software, and policies. The skill level required to operate a network is directly related to its complexity. A large enterprise, for instance, may have thousands of nodes and extensive security requirements, such as end-to-end encryption, prompting the supervision of specialized network administrators. In a nutshell, networking technology has revolutionized the world and created a new arena for the overall development of all regions.

Cisco Certifications

Cisco Systems, Inc. is a worldwide technological leader in networking and communications products and services. The company's commercial switching and routing technologies, which direct data, voice, and video traffic across networks worldwide, are undoubtedly its most well-known products.

You will need Cisco certification training courses to succeed in the CCNA, CCNP, or CCENT exam. You will need Cisco certification training courses to pass the CCNA, CCNP, or CCENT exam.

Cisco's training and certification programs have been updated to reflect today's dynamic technologies and to prepare students, engineers, and software developers for the most vital roles in the industry.

Cisco certifications

Technology	Entry	Associate	Professional	Expert
	Use this as a starting point if you're interested in a career as a networking professional.	Master the essentials needed to launch a rewarding career as a networking professional and realize your potential with the latest technologies.	Select a core technology track and a focused concentration exam to customize your professional-level certification.	Become an expert in your field by earning the most prestigious certification in the technology industry.
Collaboration	CCT Collaboration		CCNP Collaboration	CCIE Collaboration
CyberOps		CyberOps Associate	CyberOps Professional	
Data Center	CCT Data Center		CCNP Data Center	CCIE Data Center
DevNet (Dev and Automation)		DevNet Associate	DevNet Professional	DevNet Expert
Design				CCDE
Enterprise	CCT Routing & Switching	CCNA	CCNP Enterprise	CCIE Enteprise Infrastructure CCIE Enterprise Wireless
Security			CCNP Security	CCIE Security
Service Provider			CCNP Service Provider	CCIE Service Provider

Cisco is The Networking Industry Leader

Cisco is a global networking company revolutionizing how people connect, communicate, and collaborate. When you hear the words "global network" or "networking," the first term that comes to mind is Cisco. Cisco is the computer networking industry's leader. As a market leader, Cisco manufactures various networking equipment currently employed in various computer networks and internet infrastructure.

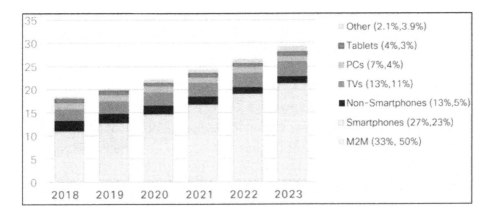

There are other vendors in the computer networking marketplace, but Cisco is by far the industry leader. Cisco controls over 50% of the network device market in several cases.

CCNA Certification

The CCNA certification validates your ability to handle the ever-changing IT market. Networking foundations, IP services, security fundamentals, automation, and programmability are all covered in the CCNA exam. CCNA confirms that you have the skills to manage and optimize the most modern networks. It is designed for agility and versatility.

The CCNA training course and exam provide a solid foundation that can prepare you to pursue various career paths in networking. The CCNA training course and exam provide a solid foundation that can prepare you to pursue various career paths in networking.

Through a CCNA certification, you will learn the following essential skills:

- Network fundamentals
- Network access
- IP connectivity
- IP services
- Security fundamentals

9

- Automation and programmability

Why should you get CCNA certification?

The CCNA provides a solid knowledge basis and current and comprehensive skillsets for a successful career. It is the cornerstone for a successful IT career that includes other certifications.

Even as technology evolves, a Cisco CCNA Routing and Switching certification offers you the knowledge and expertise to excel in networking. The course CCNA will teach you how to set up, monitor, and troubleshoot network infrastructure items at the heart of the IoT (Internet of Things).

How does CCNA help an IT Engineer?

Networking is a large and intricate field with many theories and practical work that needs a lot of effort and time to master. Despite this, only a few universities provide specific networking courses, with the majority opting to cover the subject alongside other subjects. Beginning with the necessary gear you will encounter in this sector, the CCNA gives an engineer everything they need to work in a busy server room.

As Cisco is one of the world's leading networking firms, employers will immediately recognize this certification. It is mandatory for anyone seeking an entry-level position in this sector.

Exam Information

Prior Certification Not Required		Exam Validity 3 Years	
Exam Fee $300 USD		Exam Duration 120 Minutes	
No. of Questions 60		Passing Marks 825 out of 1000	
Recommended Experience Foundational knowledge of Computer and Networking			
Exam Format Multiple Choice, Drag & drop, Case studies, Multiple Response			

The Advantages of a CCNA Certificate

Certifications provide advantages, especially if you choose a practical career like networking. On the other hand, the CCNA system from Cisco gives a lot more than other certifications, and you can see some real examples of the benefits below.

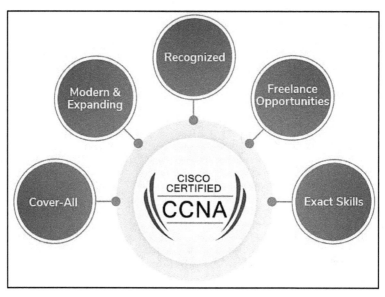

Covers the Complete Domain

The CCNA is intended to be a one-stop shop for novice network engineers. It means you will have all the skills you need to start working as soon as you pass without requiring more information to catch up.

Modern and Expanding

Cisco puts a lot of effort into keeping its certifications current, and the CCNA is no different. CCNA certification is always applicable. It covers the OSI model and TCP/IP and is updated to meet new hardware and techniques.

Recognized

Employers worldwide will recognize CCNA, and many of them will require it. It makes it easier to get employment once you have completed your education, even while others have difficulty.

Freelance Opportunities

Adopting the CCNA as the foundation for a freelancing career is a viable option. For example, a Field Engineer may be able to assist you in this by allowing you to locate freelance jobs based on your certifications.

Exact Skills

Unlike other networking courses, the CCNA will cover all networking aspects, including hardware and software. A CCNA certification is essential for anyone interested in working in this profession, as employers demand professionals with diverse abilities.

Benefits of CCNA Certification and Acquired Expertise:

CCNA training provides many skills, such as troubleshooting, configuring and monitoring, IP addressing, and network management. It also provides communication, organizational, and analytical skills.

The following are the key benefits:

- Good command of switching and routing skills
- Knowledge of LAN technologies, Switches, Cables, Bridges
- A firm foundation for networking technology
- Grasp over Inter-VLAN routing
- Understanding of IP technology and LAN switch technology
- Expertise in troubleshooting and WAN technology

CCNA Certification - Career Benefits:

- Enhances team management and collaboration skills.
- It helps in acquiring better jobs in the networking field
- Provides a firm base in the field that makes an individual self-confident
- It helps demonstrate the applicant's proficiency in the field

Prerequisites

There are no test prerequisites; however, according to Cisco, CCNA candidates should have the following experience before taking the exam:

- At least a year of experience with Cisco products and solutions
- Knowledge of IP addressing

13

- Basic understanding of network concepts

Recertification

After the date of issue, your certification is valid for three years. You must meet a number of recertification requirements in order to recertify before your certificate expires. You do not need to take any action to maintain your CCNA certification. Cisco is renowned for often updating its certification scheme.

Option for Exams and Continuing Education (CE)

You can earn 30 CE credits by passing the CCNA exam.

You must retake the exam to obtain active status and recertify. Earning the subsequent level of certificates, continuing education credits, or both during the active time will qualify you to apply for recertification.

Practice Questions

1. Which protocols are examples of TCP/IP transport layer protocols?
A. Ethernet
B. UDP
C. TCP
D. Option B and C

2. Which protocols are examples of TCP/IP data-link layer protocols?
A. Ethernet
B. HTTP
C. PPP
D. Option B and C

3. The process of HTTP asking TCP to send some data and making sure that it is received correctly is an example of what?
A. Same-layer interaction
B. Adjacent-layer interaction
C. OSI model
D. All of these answers are correct

4. The process of TCP on one computer marking a TCP segment as segment 1, and the receiving computer then acknowledging the receipt of TCP segment 1 is an example of what?
A. Data encapsulation
B. Same-layer interaction
C. Adjacent-layer interaction
D. OSI model

5. The process of a web server adding a TCP header to the contents of a web page, followed by adding an IP header and then adding a data-link header and trailer, is an example of what?
A. Data encapsulation

B. Same-layer interaction

C. OSI model

D. All of these answers are correct

6. Which of the following terms is used specifically to identify the entity created when encapsulating data inside data-link layer headers and trailers?

A. Data

B. Chunk

C. Segment

D. Frame

7. Which OSI encapsulation term can be used instead of the term frame?

A. Layer 1 PDU

B. Layer 2 PDU

C. Layer 3 PDU

D. Layer 5 PDU

8. What does a networking model mainly define?

A. A set of logical rules for communication

B. Physical requirements for networking

C. How each part of the network should work together

D. All of the above

9. What is the primary networking model in use today?

A. OSI

B. SNA

C. TCP/IP

D. CATV

10. What is another name for a networking model?

A. Networking protocol

B. Networking blueprint

C. Networking software

D. Networking hardware

11. Which organization started the task of creating the OSI networking model?

A. IEEE

B. ISO

C. DoD

D. IETF

12. What was the main goal of the OSI model?

A. To create proprietary networking models for vendors

B. To standardize data networking protocols for global communication

C. To replace TCP/IP

D. To develop wireless LAN standards

13. Which competing open networking model emerged from a U.S. Department of Defense contract?

A. OSI

B. IEEE 802.11

C. TCP/IP

D. HTTP

14. By the end of the 1990s, which networking model had become the common choice?

A. OSI

B. TCP/IP

C. IEEE 802.11

D. Ethernet

15. What documents does TCP/IP use to define protocols?

A. Internet Standards (IS)

B. Requests For Comments (RFCs)

C. Technical Memorandums (TMs)

D. Networking Protocols (NPs)

16. Which layer of the TCP/IP model focuses on how to transmit bits over each individual link?

A. Application

B. Transport

C. Network

D. Physical

17. What is an example of a protocol at the TCP/IP Application layer?

A. TCP

B. IP

C. Ethernet

D. HTTP

18. Which TCP/IP layer is responsible for delivering data over the entire path from the original sending computer to the final destination computer?

A. Application

B. Transport

C. Network

D. Data Link

19. What does the HTTP protocol define?

A. How web browsers can pull the contents of a web page from a web server

B. How to deliver data across a network

C. How to establish a wireless LAN connection

D. How to encode data for transmission

20. What service does the TCP transport layer protocol provide to the application layer?

A. Data encryption

B. Address resolution

C. Error recovery

D. Data compression

21. Which layer of the TCP/IP model includes the Internet Protocol (IP)?

A. Application Layer

B. Transport Layer

C. Network Layer

D. Data-Link Layer

22. What is the main function of the Internet Protocol (IP) in the TCP/IP model?
A. Data encryption
B. Addressing and routing
C. Error checking
D. Flow control

23. Which device is responsible for forwarding packets of data to the correct destination in a TCP/IP network?
A. Switch
B. Router
C. Hub
D. Network Interface Card (NIC)

24. What does the term 'IP host' refer to in the context of TCP/IP networking?
A. Any device connected to a TCP/IP network
B. A dedicated IP server
C. Any device that does not use IP
D. Only routers

25. In the analogy comparing IP to the postal service, what do the lower layers of the TCP/IP model represent?
A. The person sending the letter
B. The Mailbox
C. The postal service infrastructure
D. The stamps

26. In the given example, what is the IP address format used?
A. Binary notation
B. Hexadecimal notation
C. Dotted-decimal notation
D. Octal notation

27. What does a router do when it receives an IP packet?
A. Modifies the IP address
B. Encrypts the packet
C. Forwards the packet based on the destination IP address
D. Deletes the packet

28. Which protocol is NOT included in the transport layer of the TCP/IP model?
A. TCP
B. UDP
C. IP
D. None of the above

29. In the routing example, what does Larry's IP process do when it needs to send a packet?
A. Sends the packet directly to Bob
B. Chooses to send the packet to a nearby router
C. Encrypts the packet
D. Drops the packet

30. What is the role of the data-link layer in the TCP/IP model?
A. Defines how data is transmitted across the physical network
B. Manages application data
C. Handles IP addressing
D. Provides end-to-end communication

31. Which layer in the TCP/IP model is responsible for encapsulating application data with any required application layer headers?
A. Physical layer
B. Data-link layer
C. Transport layer
D. Application layer

32. What is the correct order of the encapsulation process in the TCP/IP model?
A. Application, Physical, Network, Transport, Data-link

B. Application, Transport, Network, Data-link, Physical

C. Transport, Application, Network, Data-link, Physical

D. Physical, Data-link, Network, Transport, Application

33. What term is used to refer to a message at the transport layer in the TCP/IP model?

A. Frame

B. Packet

C. Segment

D. Data

34. At which step of the TCP/IP encapsulation process is the data transmitted as bits?

A. Step 1

B. Step 2

C. Step 4

D. Step 5

35. In the OSI model, what layer number corresponds to the network layer?

A. Layer 2

B. Layer 3

C. Layer 4

D. Layer 5

36. Which of the following is NOT a function of the data-link layer?

A. Physical transmission of data

B. Error detection

C. Logical Addressing

D. Flow control

37. What is encapsulated by the Ethernet link layer?

A. HTTP headers

B. TCP headers

C. IP packets

D. Application data

38. What term is used to refer to a message at the network layer in the OSI model?
A. Frame
B. Packet
C. Segment
D. Protocol Data Unit (PDU)

39. What is the purpose of a trailer in the data-link layer?
A. To encapsulate the network layer header
B. To encapsulate the transport layer header
C. To provide error detection and correction
D. To encapsulate the application layer data

40. Which TCP/IP layer's function is equivalent to the OSI physical layer?
A. Application layer
B. Transport layer
C. Data-link layer
D. Physical layer

41. Which of the following Ethernet standards defines Gigabit Ethernet over UTP cabling?
A. 10GBASE-T
B 100BASE-T
C. 1000BASE-T
D. None of the other answers is correct.

42. In the LAN for a small office, some user devices connect to the LAN using a cable, while others connect using wireless technology (and no cable). Which of the following is true regarding the use of Ethernet in this LAN?
A. Only the devices that use cables are using Ethernet.
B. Only the devices that use wireless are using Ethernet.
C. Both the devices using cables and those using wireless are using Ethernet.
D. None of the devices are using Ethernet.

43. Which of the following is true about Ethernet crossover cables for Fast Ethernet?

A. Pins 1 and 2 are reversed on the other end of the cable.

B. Pins 1 and 2 on one end of the cable connect to pins 3 and 6 on the other end of the cable.

C. Pins 1 and 2 on one end of the cable connect to pins 3 and 4 on the other end of the cable.

D. The cable can be up to 1000 meters long to cross over between buildings.

44. Which of the following protocols is used to find the MAC address of a device from its IP address?

A. DNS

B. ARP

C. DHCP

D. ICMP

45. Which of the following are the advantages of using multimode fiber for an Ethernet link instead of UTP or single-mode fiber?

A. To achieve the longest distance possible for that single link.

B. To extend the link beyond 100 meters while keeping initial costs as low as possible.

C. To make use of an existing stock of laser-based SFP/SFP+ modules.

D. To make use of an existing stock of LED-based SFP/SFP+ modules.

46. Which of the following is true about the CSMA/CD algorithm?

A. The algorithm never allows collisions to occur.

B. Collisions can happen, but the algorithm defines how the computers should notice a collision and how to recover.

C. The algorithm works with only two devices on the same Ethernet.

D. None of the other answers is correct.

47. Which of the following is true about the Ethernet FCS field?

A. Ethernet uses FCS for error recovery.

B. It is 2 bytes long.

C. It resides in the Ethernet trailer, not the Ethernet header.

D. It is used for encryption.

48. Which configuration command enables a switch to be manageable from a remote location using SSH?
A. enable secret cisco
B. ip domain-name example.com
C. crypto key generate rsa
D. line vty 0 4

49. What is the primary purpose of the ip dhcp snooping command on a switch?
A. To provide DHCP services to hosts on the network.
B. To prevent unauthorized DHCP servers from providing IP addresses.
C. To enable DHCP relay services.
D. To monitor DHCP traffic for troubleshooting purposes.

50. What devices do SOHO networks often use to combine the functionality of a router and an Ethernet switch?
A. Ethernet hub
B. Wireless access point
C. Wireless router
D. Repeater

51. Which IEEE standard number is common to all Ethernet standards?
A. 802.11
B. 802.3
C. 802.15
D. 802.1X

52. What type of cabling does 1000BASE-T use?
A. Fiber, 5000 m
B. Copper, 100 m
C. Fiber, 100 m
D. Copper, 5000 m

53. Which encoding scheme does Ethernet use to send data over UTP cables?

A. Binary Coded Decimal

B. Manchester Encoding

C. 10BASE-T Encoding

D. Twisted Pair Encoding

54. What is the maximum length for a 10BASE-T Ethernet cable?

A. 100 m

B. 500 m

C. 5000 m

D. 10000 m

55. What is the primary advantage of using fiber-optic cabling over UTP cabling?

A. Lower cost

B. Longer cabling distances

C. Easier to install

D. More flexible

56. What is the informal IEEE standard name for Gigabit Ethernet using fiber cabling?

A. 1000BASE-T

B. 1000BASE-LX

C. 1000BASE-SX

D. 1000BASE-CX

57. What is the purpose of twisting pairs of wires in a UTP cable?

A. To make the cable more flexible

B. To reduce electromagnetic interference (EMI)

C. To increase the speed of data transmission

D. To make the cable easier to manufacture

58. What type of connector is commonly used with UTP Ethernet cables?

A. RJ-11

B. RJ-45

C. BNC

D. SC

59. What is the maximum speed defined for Ethernet standards as of the given text?

A. 10 Gbps

B. 100 Gbps

C. 400 Gbps

D. 1 Tbps

60. What does the Ethernet data-link layer protocol focus on?

A. Sending bits over a cable

B. Encoding schemes

C. Sending Ethernet frames from source to destination

D. Twisting wire pairs

61. Which type of transceiver is used on 10-Gbps interfaces?

A. GBIC

B. SFP

C. SFP+

D.UTP

62. What is the main difference between SFP and SFP+?

A. SFP+ is larger

B. SFP+ supports higher speeds

C. SFP is used for 10-Gbps interfaces

D. SFP+ is used for fiber optic cable only

63. Which pin pairs do PC NICs use to transmit data in a 10BASE-T or 100BASE-T network?

A. Pins 1 and 2

B. Pins 3 and 6

C. Pins 1 and 3

D. Pins 2 and 6

64. What type of cable is required to connect two switches in a 10BASE-T

VERSAtile Reads

or 100BASE-T network?

A. Straight-through cable

B. Crossover cable

C. Fiber optic cable

D. Coaxial cable

65. How many wire pairs does 1000BASE-T use?

A. 2

B. 3

C. 4

D. 5

66. What is the primary reason for using fiber cabling in an Ethernet LAN?

A. It is cheaper than UTP

B. It can reach greater distances

C. It is easier to install

D. It uses fewer wire pairs

67. Which cable pinout is used when a PC is connected to a switch in a 10BASE-T or 100BASE-T network?

A. Crossover cable pinout

B. Straight-through cable pinout

C. Fiber optic cable pinout

D. Coaxial cable pinout

68. What feature allows Cisco switches to automatically adjust when the wrong cable is used?

A. Auto-detect

B. Auto-configure

C. Auto-mdix

D. Auto-switch

69. Which devices transmit on pins 3 and 6 in a 10BASE-T or 100BASE-T network?

A. PC NICs

B. Hubs

C. Routers

D. Switches

70. What additional pin pairs are used in the Gigabit Ethernet crossover cable that are not used in the 10BASE-T or 100BASE-T crossover cable?
A. Pins 1 and 2
B. Pins 3 and 6
C. Pins 4 and 5, and 7 and 8
D. Pins 5 and 7

71. Which material is primarily used in fiber-optic cabling?
A. Plastic
B. Copper
C. Glass
D. Aluminum

72. What is the function of the cladding in a fiber-optic cable?
A. To transmit light
B. To reflect light into the core
C. To provide strength to the cable
D. To protect the outer jacket

73. Which type of fiber-optic cable uses multiple angles (modes) of light waves?
A. Single-mode fiber
B. Multimode fiber
C. Duplex fiber
D. Simplex fiber

74. What type of transmitter is used with single-mode fiber?
A. LED-based transmitter
B. Laser-based transmitter
C. Infrared transmitter
D. Electromagnetic transmitter

75. What is the maximum distance for 10GBASE-LR over single-mode fiber

without repeaters?

A. 100m

B. 300m

C. 10km

D. 30km

76. Which type of cabling is most susceptible to electromagnetic interference (EMI)?

A. UTP

B. Multimode fiber

C. Single-mode fiber

D. Coaxial cable

77. Which type of fiber optic cable allows distances into the tens of kilometers?

A. UTP

B. Multimode fiber

C. Single-mode fiber

D. Coaxial cable

78. What is the relative cost of switch ports for single-mode fiber compared to UTP?

A. Lower

B. Similar

C. Higher

D. It depends on the manufacturer

79. What is a key benefit of using fiber-optic cables in highly secure networks?

A. Lower cost

B. Less susceptibility to EMI

C. No emissions that can be copied

D. Easier installation

80. In the context of Ethernet cabling, what does "SFP" stand for?

A. Small Form-factor Pluggable

B. Single Fiber Port

C. Secure Fiber Protocol

D. Speedy Fiber Plug

81. What is the length of a MAC address in bytes?

A. 4 bytes

B. 6 bytes

C. 8 bytes

D. 10 bytes

82. Which organization assigns a universally unique 3-byte code to manufacturers for MAC addresses?

A. IETF

B. IEEE

C. ISO

D. ANSI

83. What term is used to refer to a MAC address that represents a single LAN interface?

A. Broadcast address

B. Unicast address

C. Multicast address

D. Group address

84. What is the value of the Ethernet broadcast address?

A. 0000.0000.0000

B. FFFF.FFFF.FFFF

C. 1111.1111.1111

D. ABCD.EFGH.IJKL

85. Which field in the Ethernet frame helps in identifying the type of network layer packet inside the frame?

A. Source Address

B. Destination Address

C. Type Field

D. Frame Check Sequence (FCS)

86. What is the main purpose of the Frame Check Sequence (FCS) field in an Ethernet frame?
A. Error detection
B. Error recovery
C. Frame forwarding
D. Address resolution

87. What happens to an Ethernet frame if an error is detected in the FCS field?
A. The frame is corrected and forwarded
B. The frame is discarded
C. The frame is sent back to the sender
D. The frame is stored for later analysis

88. What term does IEEE use to emphasize the uniqueness of a MAC address assigned by a manufacturer?
A. Burned-in address
B. Physical address
C. Universal address
D. Hardware address

89. Which addresses identify more than one LAN interface card?
A. Unicast addresses
B. Broadcast addresses
C. Multicast addresses
D. Group addresses

90. Which of the following is NOT a common name for an Ethernet address?
A. LAN address
B. Burned-in address
C. IP address
D. Physical address

91. Which of the following statements best describes a full duplex in networking?
A. The device must wait to send if it is currently receiving a frame.
B. The device does not have to wait before sending; it can send and receive at the same time.
C. The device forwards data using physical layer standards.
D. The device operates as a Layer 1 device.

92. What behavior is associated with half-duplex communication?
A. The device can send and receive data at the same time.
B. The device must wait to send if it is currently receiving a frame.
C. The device forwards data using data-link standards.
D. The device does not need to use CSMA/CD.

93. What type of device was commonly used before Ethernet switches and provided a number of RJ-45 ports for connecting PCs?
A. LAN switch
B. Router
C. LAN hub
D. Wireless access point

94. Which of the following is a characteristic of LAN hubs?
A. They forward data using data-link layer standards.
B. They look at MAC addresses to make forwarding decisions.
C. They repeat incoming electrical signals out of all other ports.
D. They operate as Layer 3 devices.

95. Why are collisions more likely to happen in networks using LAN hubs?
A. Because hubs use full-duplex logic.
B. Because hubs use half-duplex logic.
C. Because hubs repeat all received electrical signals, even if multiple are received at the same time.
D. Because hubs look at MAC addresses to make forwarding decisions.

96. What does CSMA/CD stand for?
A. Carrier Sense Multiple Access with Collision Detection

B. Carrier Sense Multiple Access with Collision Division

C. Carrier Sense Multiple Access with Collision Distribution

D. Carrier Sense Multiple Access with Collision Duplication

97. Which of the following statements is true about Ethernet point-to-point links?

A. They require CSMA/CD.

B. They share the network bandwidth among all devices connected.

C. Each link works independently of the others.

D. They use half-duplex logic.

98. In which scenario should a network interface card (NIC) and a switch port use half duplex?

A. When connected to a LAN switch.

B. When connected to a LAN hub.

C. When connected to a router.

D. When connected to a wireless access point.

99. What happens when two devices transmit a signal at the same instant in a network using a LAN hub?

A. The hub queues the signals and sends them sequentially.

B. The hub forwards both signals to their respective destinations without issue.

C. The signals collide and become garbled.

D. The signals are converted into frames and sent out.

100. What does the term 'Ethernet-shared media' refer to?

A. Designs that use switches and work independently of others.

B. Designs that use hubs, require CSMA/CD, and share the bandwidth.

C. Designs that use routers to manage network traffic.

D. Designs that use wireless access points to share the network.

101. Which command is used to set the enable secret password to "love" on a Cisco switch?

A. enable password love

B. enable secret love

C. enable password secret love

D. enable configure love

102. What command is used to enter console configuration mode on a Cisco switch?

A. line vty 0 15

B. line console 0

C. configure terminal

D. enable secret

103. What is the password set for the console line in the example?

A. love

B. hope

C. faith

D. trust

104. Which command allows Telnet users to log in with the password "hope"?

A. line vty 0 4 password hope login

B. line console 0 password hope login

C. enable secret hope

D. line vty 0 15 password hope login

105. How many vty lines are configured on the switch in the example?

A. 0

B. 4

C. 5

D. 16

106. Which command is used to configure the switch to prompt for both username and password for Telnet users?

A. login

B. login local

C. enable secret

D. password

107. What command removes any existing simple shared passwords for good housekeeping of the configuration file?
A. no password
B. delete password
C. clear password
D. unset password

108. What is the purpose of the command `crypto key generate rsa`?
A. To set the console password
B. To generate SSH encryption keys
C. To configure Telnet access
D. To reset the switch

109. What default setting allows both SSH and Telnet on the vty lines?
A. transport input all
B. transport input none
C. transport input telnet ssh
D. transport input ssh

110. Which command is used to configure the default gateway on a Cisco switch?
A. ip gateway default
B. ip route default
C. ip default-gateway
D. ip address default

111. What does subnetting involve?
A. Combining multiple networks into a single network
B. Dividing a large network into smaller, more manageable subnets
C. Changing the IP address format
D. Converting IPv4 addresses to IPv6

112. What is a Class B network address for 172.16.0.0?
A. 172.16.0.0 to 172.16.0.255
B. 172.16.0.0 to 172.16.255.255
C. 172.16.0.0 to 172.16.1.255

D. 172.16.0.0 to 172.16.255.0

113. What is the main purpose of subnetting in IP networking?
A. To increase the number of available IP addresses
B. To improve network security
C. To divide a large network into smaller, more efficient subnets
D. To change the IP address format

114. What does the term "subnet" stand for?
A. Subordinate network
B. Subdivided network
C. Super network
D. Subordinate net mask

115. How does subnetting help in network design?
A. It reduces the number of routers required
B. It allows for more efficient use of IP addresses
C. It increases the speed of the network
D. It simplifies network configuration

116. At what point can an ACL be applied to an interface on a Cisco router?
A. Inbound
B. Outbound
C. Both inbound and outbound
D. Neither inbound nor outbound

117. Which hosts should be grouped together into a subnet?
A. Hosts that are in different geographic locations
B. Hosts that are not separated by a router
C. Hosts that use different network protocols
D. Hosts that do not need to communicate with each other

118. How many subnets are required for an internetwork with four VLANs and three point-to-point serial links?
A. 4
B. 3

C. 7

D. 1

119. What is the primary reason for using different subnet sizes in a network design?
A. To make the network easier to manage
B. To waste fewer IP addresses
C. To increase the number of available subnets
D. To improve network security

120. What command is used to enter the configuration mode on a Cisco switch?
A. enable
B. configure terminal
C. switchport mode
D. vlan database

121. Which command dynamically creates a VLAN when assigning a port to it?
A. vlan create
B. switchport access vlan
C. vlan vlan-id
D. access vlan create

122. What is the default name assigned by a switch when it creates VLAN 3?
A. VLAN03
B. VLAN0003
C. VLAN3
D. Default-VLAN3

123. What is the purpose of the VLAN Trunking Protocol (VTP)?
A. To advertise VLAN configurations to other switches
B. To create VLANs dynamically
C. To secure VLAN configurations
D. To speed up VLAN configuration

124. Which VTP mode effectively disables VTP?
A. Client
B. Server
C. Transparent
D. Dynamic

125. Which command is used to disable VTP completely on some switches?
A. vtp mode client
B. vtp mode server
C. vtp mode transparent
D. vtp mode off

126. What command can you use to check VTP status on a switch?
A. show vlan
B. show vtp status
C. show vlan brief
D. show interfaces trunk

127. Which type of trunking is supported by most modern Cisco switches?
A. ISL
B. 802.1Q
C. VTP
D. DTP

128. What command sets a switch port to always act as an access port?
A. switchport mode access
B. switchport mode trunk
C. switchport mode dynamic
D. switchport mode negotiate

129. Which command sets a switch port to always act as a trunk port?
A. switchport mode access
B. switchport mode trunk
C. switchport mode dynamic
D. switchport mode negotiate

130. What is the default administrative mode for trunking on a Cisco 2960 switch?
A. dynamic desirable
B. dynamic auto
C. access
D. trunk

131. Which command initiates trunk negotiation messages?
A. switchport mode access
B. switchport mode trunk
C. switchport mode dynamic desirable
D. switchport nonegotiate

132. What administrative mode means a switch port will only respond to trunk negotiation messages?
A. access
B. trunk
C. dynamic desirable
D. dynamic auto

133. Which command disables DTP negotiations on a port?
A. switchport mode access
B. switchport mode dynamic desirable
C. switchport nonegotiate
D. switchport mode trunk

134. What is the purpose of the 'show interfaces trunk' command?
A. To display all configured VLANs
B. To display trunk information on operational trunk ports
C. To display VTP status
D. To display VLAN brief details

135. What mode should you avoid configuring on one end as 'access' and the other end as 'trunk'?
A. Dynamic auto
B. Dynamic desirable

C. Access and trunk

D. Transparent

136. Which VLAN is used as the default native VLAN?
A. VLAN 1
B. VLAN 1002
C. VLAN 1005
D. VLAN 2

137. What can happen if you change VTP settings on a switch connected to the production network?
A. Improve network performance
B. Cause VLAN configuration changes across the network
C. Disable VLANs
D. Secure the network

138. What is the command output if no interfaces are operationally trunking?
A. No output
B. List of all VLANs
C. List of all interfaces
D. Error message

139. What administrative mode should be set to ensure a switch port always acts as a non-trunk port?
A. switchport mode access
B. switchport mode trunk
C. switchport mode dynamic
D. switchport mode negotiate

140. Which command is used to view the VLAN configuration on a switch?
A. show vlan
B. show interfaces switchport
C. show vlan brief
D. show interfaces trunk

141. What does the 'switchport access vlan' command do if the VLAN does not exist?
A. Creates the VLAN
B. Shows an error
C. Ignores the command
D. Deletes the VLAN

142. What does VTP Transparent mode allow?
A. Configuring standard and extended-range VLANs
B. Learning VLANs from other switches
C. Advertising VLANs to other switches
D. Configuring only standard VLANs

143. What is the result of configuring 'switchport mode dynamic auto' on both ends of a link?
A. Always trunk
B. Always access
C. May or may not trunk
D. Never trunk

144. What does 'switchport mode dynamic desirable' do?
A. Initiates trunk negotiation
B. Waits for trunk negotiation
C. Always trunks
D. Always access

145. Which command can be used to configure a VLAN on a switch?
A. vlan 10
B. vlan create 10
C. switchport vlan 10
D. vlan database

146. What is the default state of a VLAN when it is created automatically by a switch?
A. Active
B. Inactive

C. Suspended

D. Shutdown

147. Which command allows a switch to negotiate trunking settings?
A. switchport mode dynamic desirable
B. switchport mode dynamic auto
C. switchport nonegotiate
D. switchport mode trunk

148. What does the 'show vlan brief' command display?
A. Detailed VLAN information
B. Brief summary of VLANs and their status
C. Trunk port information
D. VTP status

149. What does the 'switchport mode trunk' command do?
A. Forces the port to become a trunk
B. Forces the port to become an access port
C. Negotiates trunking
D. Disables trunking

150. Which VLANs are supported by a switch using VTP server or client mode?
A. Extended-range VLANs only
B. Standard-range VLANs only
C. Both standard-and extended-range VLANs
D. Native VLANs only

151. What happens if a switch uses VTP client mode?
A. It can configure VLANs
B. It cannot configure VLANs
C. It advertises VLANs
D. It creates VLANs

152. What type of trunking protocol is DTP?
A. IEEE 802.1Q

B. VLAN Trunking Protocol

C. Dynamic Trunking Protocol

D. Inter-Switch Link

153. What is the default mode of a switch that supports both ISL and 802.1Q?

A. ISL

B. 802.1Q

C. Negotiate

D. Auto

154. Which command sets an administrative mode that initiates trunk negotiation and also responds to it?

A. switchport mode dynamic desirable

B. switchport mode dynamic auto

C. switchport mode access

D. switchport mode trunk

155. What is the result when one switch port is set to 'dynamic desirable' and the other to 'dynamic auto'?

A. The link will not trunk

B. The link will trunk

C. The link will become access

D. The link will fail

156. Which command is used to view the operational mode of an interface?

A. show interfaces switchport

B. show vlan brief

C. show interfaces trunk

D. show vtp status

157. What does the 'switchport nonegotiate' command do?

A. Disables DTP negotiations

B. Enables DTP negotiations

C. Forces trunking

D. Forces access mode

158. What is the effect of setting 'vtp mode off'?
A. Disables VTP completely
B. Sets VTP to client mode
C. Sets VTP to server mode
D. Enables VTP

159. Which command is used to change the VTP mode to transparent?
A. vtp mode client
B. vtp mode server
C. vtp mode transparent
D. vtp mode off

160. What does 'switchport mode dynamic desirable' configure the switch to do?
A. Always trunk
B. Wait for negotiation
C. Initiate and respond to negotiation
D. Always access

161. What command would you use to configure a port to never trunk?
A. switchport mode trunk
B. switchport mode access
C. switchport nonegotiate
D. switchport mode dynamic desirable

162. What is the default VLAN for untagged frames on an 802.1Q trunk?
A. VLAN 1
B. VLAN 1002
C. VLAN 1003
D. VLAN 1005

163. What command would you use to set a switch port to access mode?
A. switchport access vlan
B. switchport mode access
C. switchport mode trunk

D. switchport mode dynamic

164. What does the 'show vlan' command display?
A. Trunk ports
B. VLAN configurations
C. VTP status
D. Interface details

165. What is the result of configuring 'switchport mode dynamic auto' on both ends of a link?
A. Always trunks
B. Never trunks
C. May trunk if the negotiation is successful
D. Always access

166. What happens if you configure 'vtp mode transparent'?
A. The switch cannot create VLANs
B. The switch does not participate in VTP
C. The switch advertises VLANs to other switches
D. The switch learns VLANs from other switches

167. Which command sets the interface to trunk mode and then disables DTP?
A. switchport mode access
B. switchport mode trunk
C. switchport mode dynamic desirable
D. switchport nonegotiate

168. What is one of the main purposes of using VLANs in a network?
A. Increase broadcast domains
B. Decrease security
C. Segment network traffic
D. Reduce the number of switches needed

169. What is required for two switches to successfully negotiate trunking?
A. Both must be set to dynamic auto

B. One must be set to dynamic desirable
C. Both must be set to access mode
D. One must be set to trunk mode

170. What is the main purpose of STP/RSTP?
A. To improve network speed
B. To prevent looping frames
C. To enhance security
D. To manage VLAN configurations

171. How does STP/RSTP prevent looping frames?
A. By adding additional ports
B. By sending frames to a central server
C. By adding an additional check on each interface
D. By encrypting the frames

172. What happens when an interface is in the STP/RSTP blocking state?
A. It forwards and receives all user traffic
B. It blocks all user traffic and does not send or receive user traffic
C. It connects to a backup server
D. It changes to a trunk port

173. What state do interfaces in the forwarding state act as?
A. Normal, forwarding and receiving frames
B. Blocking and discarding frames
C. Learning and listening for frames
D. Disconnected, not forwarding any frames

174. What is a broadcast storm?
A. A sudden increase in network speed
B. The indefinite looping of broadcast frames
C. A network security breach
D. The failure of multiple switches simultaneously

175. Which of the following is NOT a problem caused by looping frames?
A. Broadcast storms

B. MAC table stability

C. Multiple frame transmission

D. MAC table instability

176. What does STP/RSTP use to solve the problem of looping frames?

A. Multiple VLANs

B. Additional switches

C. Blocking certain switch ports

D. Increasing bandwidth

177. What happens during a broadcast storm?

A. Frames loop indefinitely

B. Frames are encrypted

C. Frames are sent to a central server

D. Frames are deleted automatically

178. What is MAC table instability?

A. The stability of MAC addresses in a network

B. The continual updating of MAC address tables with incorrect entries

C. The removal of MAC addresses from a table

D. The addition of new MAC addresses to a table

179. What is the purpose of placing each switch port in either a forwarding or blocking state?

A. To increase network speed

B. To prevent looping frames

C. To enhance security

D. To reduce network congestion

180. What does STP/RSTP convergence refer to?

A. The process of increasing network speed

B. The process of making switches block or forward on each interface

C. The process of updating VLAN configurations

D. The process of encrypting frames

181. What does STP/RSTP create to manage network traffic?

A. A VLAN

B. A spanning tree of interfaces

C. A centralized server

D. A backup network

182. What does STP/RSTP do with interfaces that block?

A. Forward and receive user frames

B. Learn MAC addresses of received frames

C. Process received user frames

D. Ignore user frames except STP/RSTP messages

183. What is one negative side effect of STP?

A. Increased bandwidth

B. Decreased security

C. Not using the link between switches for traffic in a VLAN

D. Slower network speed

184. What happens when a port is placed in a blocking state in STP/RSTP?

A. It forwards traffic as usual

B. It does not process any frames except STP/RSTP messages

C. It connects to a backup server

D. It changes its MAC address

185. What kind of frames cause broadcast storms?

A. Encrypted frames

B. Looping Ethernet frames

C. VLAN frames

D. Trunk frames

186. Why do switches flood broadcasts out all interfaces in the same VLAN except the one where the frame arrived?

A. To increase security

B. To prevent frame looping

C. To ensure all devices receive the broadcast

D. To improve network speed

187. What does a switch do when it receives a frame with an unknown destination MAC address?
A. Drops the frame
B. Encrypts the frame
C. Floods the frame out all interfaces
D. Sends the frame to a central server

188. What is a side effect of looping frames?
A. Increased network speed
B. Multiple copies of one frame being delivered to the intended host
C. Enhanced security
D. Improved MAC table stability

189. When does STP/RSTP convergence occur?
A. When the network speed increases
B. When something changes in the LAN topology
C. When new devices are added to the network
D. When VLAN configurations are updated

190. What does STP/RSTP do when a network outage occurs?
A. Sends frames to a backup server
B. Encrypts all frames
C. Converges to change state from blocking to forwarding
D. Deletes all frames

191. What role do bridges play in STP/RSTP?
A. They encrypt frames
B. They connect LANs and implement STP/RSTP
C. They increase network speed
D. They manage VLAN configurations

192. What is the primary function of STP/RSTP?
A. To manage VLAN configurations
B. To prevent loops in Ethernet LANs
C. To enhance network security
D. To increase network speed

193. What state do interfaces in the blocking state act as?
A. Normal, forwarding and receiving frames
B. Blocking and discarding frames
C. Learning and listening for frames
D. Disconnected, not forwarding any frames

194. What happens to the switch's MAC address table during a broadcast storm?
A. It becomes more accurate
B. It remains stable
C. It gets continually updated with incorrect entries
D. It gets deleted

195. What does a switch think when it receives a frame with the same source MAC on different ports?
A. The frame is corrupted
B. The source MAC has moved to a different port
C. The frame should be dropped
D. The frame should be encrypted

196. What does STP/RSTP do to prevent loops?
A. Increases network speed
B. Blocks certain switch ports
C. Encrypts frames
D. Updates VLAN configurations

197. How does STP/RSTP handle interfaces that block?
A. Forward and receive user frames
B. Learn MAC addresses of received frames
C. Process received user frames
D. Ignore user frames except STP/RSTP messages

198. What is one problem that occurs when STP/RSTP is not used?
A. Increased network speed
B. Enhanced security

C. Looping frames causing network congestion

D. Improved MAC table stability

199. What is the result of MAC table instability?

A. Frames being sent to the correct locations

B. Frames being sent to the wrong locations

C. Increased network speed

D. Enhanced security

200. What does STP/RSTP do to handle network outages?

A. Sends frames to a backup server

B. Encrypts all frames

C. Converges to change state from blocking to forwarding

D. Deletes all frames

201. What do interfaces in the forwarding state do?

A. Ignore user frames

B. Forward and receive frames as normal

C. Block all user traffic

D. Connect to a backup server

202. What is the purpose of a spanning tree in STP/RSTP?

A. To increase network speed

B. To manage VLAN configurations

C. To create a single path to and from each Ethernet link

D. To enhance security

203. What happens to frames during a broadcast storm?

A. They loop indefinitely

B. They are encrypted

C. They are sent to a central server

D. They are deleted automatically

204. Which command would you use to configure a switch to be the root bridge for VLAN 10?

A. spanning-tree vlan 10 priority 4096

B. spanning-tree vlan 10 root primary

C. spanning-tree vlan 10 root secondary

D. spanning-tree vlan 10 cost 4096

205. What does the command router ospf 1 followed by network 192.168.1.0 0.0.0.255 area 0 accomplish in OSPF configuration?

A. It enables OSPF on all interfaces in the 192.168.1.0/24 network.

B. It assigns the 192.168.1.0/24 network to area 1.

C. It enables OSPF on the interface with the IP address 192.168.1.0.

D. It assigns the 192.168.1.0/24 network to area 0

206. What is the primary function of STP/RSTP?

A. To manage VLAN configurations

B. To prevent loops in Ethernet LANs

C. To enhance network security

D. To increase network speed

207. What state do interfaces in the blocking state act as?

A. Normal, forwarding and receiving frames

B. Blocking and discarding frames

C. Learning and listening for frames

D. Disconnected, not forwarding any frames

208. What happens to the switch's MAC address table during a broadcast storm?

A. It becomes more accurate

B. It remains stable

C. It gets continually updated with incorrect entries

D. It gets deleted

209. What does a switch think when it receives a frame with the same source MAC on different ports?

A. The frame is corrupted

B. The source MAC has moved to a different port

C. The frame should be dropped

D. The frame should be encrypted

210. What does STP/RSTP do to prevent loops?

A. Increases network speed

B. Blocks certain switch ports

C. Encrypts frames

D. Updates VLAN configurations

211. In which HSRP state does a router send periodic hello messages to indicate its presence?

A. Standby

B. Active

C. Init

D. Listen

212. What effect does the **no ip classless** command have on a router?

A. It enables classful routing behavior.

B. It enables classless routing behavior.

C. It enables OSPF routing protocol.

D. It enables EIGRP routing protocol

213. What does the command **ip sla 1** followed by **icmp-echo 10.1.1.1** accomplish?

A. It creates an SLA operation to send ICMP echo requests to IP 10.1.1.1.

B. It sets up an SNMP trap for IP 10.1.1.1.

C. It configures a static route to IP 10.1.1.1.

D. It configures a NAT translation for IP 10.1.1.1.

214. Which type of OSPF network type requires the election of a DR/BDR?

A. Point-to-point

B. Broadcast

C. Point-to-multipoint

D. Non-broadcast

215. Which protocol does OSPF use to send link-state updates?

A. TCP

B. UDP

C. ICMP

D. IP

216. What is the effect of the **switchport mode dynamic auto** command on a switch port?

A. It makes the port a permanent trunk port.

B. It makes the port a permanent access port.

C. It negotiates trunking with the other port using DTP.

D. It disables trunking on the port.

217. Which command is used to redistribute OSPF routes into EIGRP?

A. redistribute ospf into eigrp

B. redistribute ospf

C. network ospf into eigrp

D. redistribute protocol ospf

218. Which of the following describes the main difference between TACACS+ and RADIUS?

A. TACACS+ encrypts the entire payload, while RADIUS only encrypts the password.

B. TACACS+ uses UDP, while RADIUS uses TCP.

C. TACACS+ is an open standard, while RADIUS is proprietary.

D. TACACS+ is used for remote access, while RADIUS is used for local access.

219. What does the **ip ospf dead-interval** command configure?

A. The interval between OSPF Hello packets.

B. The time an OSPF router waits to declare a neighbor down.

C. The OSPF router ID.

D. The maximum time to wait for an OSPF database description.

220. What state does STP/RSTP place interfaces not chosen to be in a forwarding state?

A. Disconnected

B. Forwarding

C. Blocking

D. Listening

221. What is the main purpose of using STP/RSTP in a network?
A. To increase the speed of data transmission
B. To prevent looping frames
C. To reduce the number of switches in a network
D. To increase the number of VLANs

222. Which switch ports are placed in a forwarding state on the root switch?
A. Only the root port
B. Only the designated port
C. All working interfaces
D. None

223. What is the term used for the switch with the lowest root cost on a link?
A. Root switch
B. Designated switch
C. Backup switch
D. Primary switch

224. What problem does STP/RSTP primarily aim to prevent in Ethernet LANs?
A. Slow data transmission
B. Unauthorized access
C. Broadcast storms
D. IP address conflicts

225. What happens when a switch interface is in a blocking state?
A. It forwards frames as usual
B. It only forwards STP/RSTP messages
C. It forwards only unicast frames
D. It forwards multicast frames

226. What is MAC table instability?

A. When MAC addresses do not change

B. When MAC address tables keep changing due to looping frames

C. When MAC addresses are duplicated

D. When MAC addresses are lost

227. What is the purpose of the Hello BPDU in STP/RSTP?

A. To send data frames

B. To transmit error messages

C. To maintain the STP/RSTP topology

D. To increase data transmission speed

228. Which two fields make up the Bridge ID (BID) in STP/RSTP?

A. Priority and VLAN ID

B. Priority and MAC address

C. VLAN ID and MAC address

D. MAC address and IP address

229. What happens if a tie occurs in the STP root election based on priority?

A. The switch with the highest MAC address wins

B. The switch with the lowest MAC address wins

C. The election is rerun

D. Both switches become root switches

230. How often does the root switch send a new Hello BPDU by default?

A. Every 1 second

B. Every 2 seconds

C. Every 5 seconds

D. Every 10 seconds

231. What is the designated port (DP) in STP/RSTP?

A. The port with the highest cost

B. The port with the lowest cost

C. The port that is blocked

D. The port that is disabled

232. Which switch port is referred to as the Root Port (RP)?
A. The port with the highest cost to the root switch
B. The port with the least cost to the root switch
C. The port with the highest priority
D. The port with the lowest priority

233. What is the main goal of STP/RSTP when choosing which ports to block?
A. To maximize data traffic
B. To prevent loops and ensure all devices can communicate
C. To increase the number of VLANs
D. To reduce the number of switches

234. What is the first step in the STP/RSTP process?
A. Electing a root switch
B. Choosing designated ports
C. Calculating root costs
D. Blocking all interfaces

235. What criteria are used by STP/RSTP to choose the root port on a non-root switch?
A. Highest MAC address
B. Lowest administrative cost to the root switch
C. Highest administrative cost to the root switch
D. Most recent connection

236. What is a broadcast storm?
A. A storm that disrupts signal transmission
B. The indefinite looping of broadcast frames in a network
C. A high volume of unicast traffic
D. A failure in the network switch

237. Why is it important for all devices in a VLAN to send frames to each other in STP/RSTP?
A. To ensure all parts of the LAN are connected
B. To increase data transmission speed

C. To decrease network congestion

D. To reduce the number of switches needed

238. What does the term "STP convergence" refer to?

A. The process of increasing data speed

B. The process of determining which ports to block and forward

C. The process of reducing the number of VLANs

D. The process of connecting more switches

239. How does STP/RSTP prevent looping frames?

A. By increasing data transmission speed

B. By adding an additional check on each interface before using it to send/receive user traffic

C. By reducing the number of switches

D. By increasing the number of VLANs

240. What happens when a switch's MAC address table keeps changing due to looping frames?

A. The switch forwards frames correctly

B. The switch forwards frames to the wrong locations

C. The switch stops forwarding frames

D. The switch increases data transmission speed

241. Which port becomes the root port on a non-root switch?

A. The port with the highest cost to the root switch

B. The port that receives the least-cost Hello BPDU from the root switch

C. The port with the highest priority

D. The port with the lowest priority

242. What is the effect of a broadcast storm on the network?

A. It increases data transmission speed

B. It significantly impacts end-user device performance

C. It reduces the number of VLANs

D. It increases the number of switches needed

243. What is the effect of blocking a port in STP/RSTP?

A. The port forwards all types of frames

B. The port does not forward user frames or learn MAC addresses

C. The port only forwards broadcast frames

D. The port only forwards multicast frames

244. When is a switch considered the designated switch on a link?

A. When it has the highest root cost

B. When it has the lowest root cost

C. When it has the highest priority

D. When it has the lowest priority

245. What happens if a switch does not receive a Hello BPDU within the expected time?

A. It continues normal operation

B. It reacts and starts the process of changing the spanning-tree topology

C. It increases data transmission speed

D. It reduces the number of VLANs

246. What is the main purpose of the Hello BPDU's root cost field?

A. To indicate the time since the last Hello BPDU

B. To indicate the switch's cost to reach the root switch

C. To indicate the switch's priority

D. To indicate the number of VLANs

247. Which switch port is placed in a forwarding state on a root switch?

A. Only the root port

B. Only the designated port

C. All working interfaces

D. None

248. What is the effect of multiple frame transmission caused by looping frames?

A. It results in a single frame being delivered to the host

B. It results in multiple copies of one frame being delivered to the host

C. It increases data transmission speed

D. It reduces the number of VLANs

249. What is the function of the sender's bridge ID field in the Hello BPDU?

A. To identify the root switch

B. To identify the switch that sent the Hello BPDU

C. To indicate the switch's cost to reach the root switch

D. To indicate the number of VLANs

250. What is the role of the designated port (DP) in STP/RSTP?

A. To block all frames

B. To forward frames onto the LAN segment

C. To increase data transmission speed

D. To reduce the number of VLANs

251. How does STP/RSTP choose the designated port on a LAN segment?

A. Based on the highest root cost

B. Based on the lowest root cost

C. Based on the highest priority

D. Based on the lowest priority

252. What is the primary reason for the root switch to place all working interfaces in a forwarding state?

A. To increase data transmission speed

B. To ensure all interfaces become designated ports (DPs)

C. To reduce the number of VLANs

D. To increase the number of switches

253. What is the function of the root port (RP) on a non-root switch?

A. To block frames

B. To forward frames to the root switch

C. To increase data transmission speed

D. To reduce the number of VLANs

254. What is the effect of a switch forwarding a Hello BPDU received from the root switch?

A. It increases data transmission speed

B. It changes the Hello to list the forwarding switch's own BID and root cost

C. It reduces the number of VLANs

D. It blocks all frames

255. What happens when a switch hears a superior Hello BPDU?
A. It continues to advertise itself as root
B. It stops advertising itself as root and forwards the superior Hello
C. It increases data transmission speed
D. It reduces the number of VLANs

256. What does STP/RSTP do if there is a tie in the root cost when choosing the root port?
A. Chooses the port with the highest neighbor bridge ID
B. Chooses the port with the lowest neighbor bridge ID
C. Chooses the port with the highest priority
D. Chooses the port with the lowest priority

257. What is the effect of a switch not receiving a Hello BPDU from the root switch?
A. It continues normal operation
B. It reacts and starts the process of changing the spanning-tree topology
C. It increases data transmission speed
D. It reduces the number of VLANs

258. What is the purpose of the root cost field in the Hello BPDU?
A. To indicate the time since the last Hello BPDU
B. To indicate the switch's cost to reach the root switch
C. To indicate the switch's priority
D. To indicate the number of VLANs

259. What is the effect of blocking a port on a switch in STP/RSTP?
A. The port forwards all types of frames
B. The port does not forward user frames or learn MAC addresses
C. The port only forwards broadcast frames
D. The port only forwards multicast frames

260. Which switch port is placed in a forwarding state on the root switch?
A. Only the root port
B. Only the designated port
C. All working interfaces
D. None

261. What is the main purpose of STP/RSTP in a network?
A. To increase the speed of data transmission
B. To prevent looping frames
C. To reduce the number of switches in a network
D. To increase the number of VLANs

262. What is the purpose of the **switchport trunk encapsulation dot1q** command on a Cisco switch?
A. To set the trunking mode to 802.1Q
B. To configure a VLAN on the trunk port
C. To enable ISL encapsulation on the trunk port
D. To disable trunking on the port

263. Which routing protocol uses multicast address 224.0.0.10 for communication?
A. OSPF
B. EIGRP
C. RIP
D. BGP

264. Which Cisco technology allows multiple physical links to be combined into a single logical link?
A. VTP
B. STP
C. EtherChannel
D. VLAN

265. What is the main function of the **DHCP snooping** feature on a switch?
A. To provide IP address allocation
B. To prevent rogue DHCP servers
C. To forward DHCP requests to the server
D. To assign static IP addresses

266. In STP, which port state is a switch port in if it can send and receive BPDUs but not forward user data?
A. Blocking
B. Listening
C. Learning
D. Forwarding

267. Which Cisco IOS command enables IPv6 routing on a router?
A. ipv6 enable
B. ipv6 routing
C. ipv6 unicast-routing
D. ipv6 address autoconfig

268. What is the effect of applying the **ip helper-address** command on a router interface?
A. It converts a broadcast to a unicast.
B. It translates IP addresses from one network to another.
C. It forwards DHCP requests to a specified DHCP server.
D. It provides NAT functionality.

269. Which command would you use to verify the EIGRP adjacencies on a router?
A. show ip eigrp neighbors
B. show ip eigrp interfaces
C. show ip eigrp topology
D. show ip eigrp routes

270. What is the result of having more host bits in a subnet mask?
A. Fewer subnets
B. More subnets
C. Larger subnets
D. Smaller subnets

271. What is the purpose of a subnet mask?
A. To define the network portion of an IP address
B. To define the host portion of an IP address
C. To determine the size of a subnet
D. All of the above

272. What is the result of using a single-size subnet in a network design?
A. Increased complexity
B. Simplified operation
C. Increased IP address waste
D. Both B and C

273. What does VLSM stand for?
A. Variable-Length Subnet Mask
B. Very Large Subnet Mask
C. Variable-Layer Subnet Mask
D. Variable-Length Super Mask

274. What is the effect of using VLSM in a network design?
A. Reduced number of subnets
B. Increased number of subnets
C. More efficient use of IP addresses
D. Both B and C

275. What is the importance of choosing the right mask for each subnet?
A. It determines the number of available IP addresses in the subnet
B. It determines the geographic location of the subnet
C. It ensures network security
D. It simplifies network configuration

276. What is the primary consideration when determining the number of hosts per subnet?
A. The number of routers in the network
B. The number of devices that need IP addresses
C. The geographic location of the subnet
D. The type of network protocol used

277. How does the engineer determine the number of subnets required for an internetwork?
A. By counting the number of hosts
B. By counting the number of routers
C. By counting the number of locations that need a subnet
D. By counting the number of IP addresses

278. What is the rule for IP addresses in the same subnet?
A. They must be separated by at least one router
B. They must not be separated by any router
C. They must use different subnet masks
D. They must use the same network protocol

279. What is the rule for IP addresses in different subnets?
A. They must be separated by at least one router
B. They must not be separated by any router
C. They must use the same subnet mask
D. They must use different network protocols

280. What is the main job of a router in a subnetted network?
A. To assign IP addresses to hosts
B. To forward packets from one subnet to another
C. To manage VLAN configurations
D. To increase network speed

281. What is the primary purpose of an Access Control List (ACL) in a Cisco router?

A. To manage router configuration

B. To filter network traffic

C. To control user access to the router

D. To monitor network performance

282. What is the impact of using private IP networks in an enterprise internetwork?

A. It reduces the number of available IP addresses

B. It increases the number of available IP addresses

C. It simplifies network configuration

D. It increases network security

283. What is the purpose of the subnet number in a subnetted network?

A. To identify the network portion of the IP address

B. To identify the host portion of the IP address

C. To identify the subnet within the network

D. To identify the geographic location of the subnet

284. What does the term "host bits" refer to in a subnet mask?

A. The bits used to define the network portion of the IP address

B. The bits used to number different host IP addresses in the subnet

C. The bits used to identify the subnet number

D. The bits used to determine the size of the subnet

285. What is the advantage of using a single-size subnet in a network design?

A. It increases the number of available IP addresses

B. It simplifies network configuration and operation

C. It improves network security

D. It reduces the number of required routers

286. What is the disadvantage of using a single-size subnet in a network design?

A. It increases network complexity

B. It wastes IP addresses

C. It reduces network security

D. It limits the number of available subnets

287. What is the primary advantage of using VLSM in a network design?
A. It simplifies network configuration
B. It allows for more efficient use of IP addresses
C. It reduces the number of required routers
D. It improves network security

288. What is the effect of using different masks for different subnets in the same Class A network?
A. It creates a simpler network design
B. It creates a more complex network design
C. It allows for more efficient use of IP addresses
D. Both B and C

289. What is the purpose of analyzing the addressing and subnetting needs of a network?
A. To determine the number of available IP addresses
B. To determine the number of required subnets and IP addresses per subnet
C. To identify the geographic location of each subnet
D. To simplify network configuration

290. What is the result of using a single mask for all subnets in a network?
A. Increased number of subnets
B. Simplified network operation
C. More efficient use of IP addresses
D. Increased network security

291. What is the first step in planning the implementation of subnets?
A. Choose DHCP ranges
B. Analyze needs
C. Assign static IP addresses
D. Configure devices

292. What should be used to keep track of which subnets are used where?
A. Network diagram

B. Subnet planning chart

C. Spreadsheet or subnet-planning tool

D. IP address list

293. Which protocol does HSRP use to provide redundancy for IP traffic?

A. ICMP

B. VRRP

C. GLBP

D. UDP

294. What feature benefits from reserving ranges of subnets based on geographic locations?

A. Static IP addressing

B. DHCP leasing

C. Route summarization

D. Network segmentation

295. In the example given, what address range is used for DHCP pools in a LAN subnet?

A. .1 through .100

B. .1 through .50

C. .101 through .254

D. .1 through .254

296. Which three of the following are required when planning the implementation of subnets?

A. Subnet locations

B. Static IP addresses

C. Network interfaces

D. DHCP Ranges

297. What is the main advantage of using a strategy for assigning subnets?

A. Reduces the number of subnets required

B. Simplifies future network expansions

C. Makes IP address tracking easier

D. Helps with route summarization

298. Which device typically uses a static IP address?
A. PC
B. Printer
C. Router
D. Mobile phone

299. What is the purpose of the network broadcast address?
A. To identify a single host
B. To communicate with all hosts in the network
C. To assign IP addresses dynamically
D. To reserve IP addresses

300. What is the default mask for a Class B network?
A. 255.0.0.0
B. 255.255.0.0
C. 255.255.255.0
D. 255.255.255.255

301. What type of IP address uses the Class D address range?
A. Unicast
B. Broadcast
C. Multicast
D. Reserved

302. Which address class is intended for large networks?
A. Class A
B. Class B
C. Class C
D. Class D

303. How many hosts per network does a Class A network support?
A. 254
B. 65,534
C. 16,777,214
D. 2,097,152

304. What is the first usable address in a network?
A. The network ID
B. One address higher than the network ID
C. The network broadcast address
D. The first address in the DHCP pool

305. What does the subnet mask 255.255.255.0 signify?
A. Class A network
B. Class B network
C. Class C network
D. Class D network

306. How many Class B networks exist?
A. 126
B. 254
C. 16,384
D. 2,097,152

307. What is the purpose of Dynamic Host Configuration Protocol (DHCP)?
A. To assign IP addresses manually
B. To configure static IP addresses
C. To dynamically lease IP addresses to hosts
D. To reserve IP addresses

308. What is the address range for a Class C network?
A. 1–126
B. 128–191
C. 192–223
D. 224–239

309. How many total hosts does a Class C network support?
A. 254
B. 65,534
C. 16,777,214

D. 2,097,152

310. What is the network part of the address in a Class B network?
A. First octet
B. First two octets
C. First three octets
D. Last octet

311. Which of the following is a reserved Class A network address?
A. 127.0.0.0
B. 128.0.0.0
C. 192.168.0.0
D. 224.0.0.0

312. How is the network broadcast address derived?
A. Change the host octets to 0
B. Change the network octets to 255
C. Change the host octets to 255
D. Change the network octets to 0

313. What is the default mask for a Class C network?
A. 255.0.0.0
B. 255.255.0.0
C. 255.255.255.0
D. 255.255.255.255

314. Which address class is used for multicast?
A. Class A
B. Class B
C. Class C
D. Class D

315. How many bits are in the network part of a Class B address?
A. 8
B. 16
C. 24

D. 32

316. What is the second step when assigning subnets to different locations?
A. Identify location
B. Assign IP addresses
C. Track the subnets used
D. Configure devices

317. What is one key factor in deciding the distribution of subnets?
A. Number of hosts
B. Location geography
C. Device type
D. IP address range

318. How many unique combinations can be made with 2 bits?
A. 2
B. 4
C. 8
D. 16

319. Which routing protocol uses the Dijkstra algorithm for calculating the shortest path?
A. OSPF
B. RIP
C. BGP
D. EIGRP

320. What is the range of valid network numbers for Class A?
A. 0.0.0.0–127.0.0.0
B. 1.0.0.0–126.0.0.0
C. 128.0.0.0–191.255.0.0
D. 192.0.0.0–223.255.255.0

321. Which of the following is an illegal binary subnet mask?
A. 11111111 11111111 00000000 00000000
B. 11111111 11111111 11111111 00001111

C. 11111111 11111111 11111111 00000000

D. 11111111 11111111 11110000 00000000

322. What is the dotted-decimal notation (DDN) for the binary subnet mask 11111111 11111111 11111111 11110000?

A. 255.255.255.0

B. 255.255.255.240

C. 255.255.255.252

D. 255.255.255.248

323. How many binary 1s are in the prefix mask /18?

A. 8

B. 16

C. 18

D. 24

324. What is the binary equivalent of the prefix mask /24?

A. 11111111 11111111 11110000 00000000

B. 11111111 11111111 11111111 00000000

C. 11111111 11111111 11111111 11110000

D. 11111111 11111111 11111000 00000000

325. How many binary 1s are in the subnet mask 255.255.192.0?

A. 16

B. 18

C. 22

D. 20

326. What is the prefix mask for binary mask 11111111 11111000 00000000 00000000?

A. /8

B. /16

C. /13

D. /24

327. What is the decimal equivalent for the binary mask 11111111 11111111

11111100 00000000?

A. 255.255.255.0

B. 255.255.255.192

C. 255.255.252.0

D. 255.255.254.0

328. Which of the following subnet masks is equivalent to /27 in dotted-decimal notation?

A. 255.255.255.0

B. 255.255.255.192

C. 255.255.255.224

D. 255.255.255.248

329. What is the prefix mask equivalent for the dotted-decimal mask 255.255.248.0?

A. /21

B. /22

C. /23

D. /24

330. Which of the following values cannot be a valid subnet mask octet?

A. 255

B. 192

C. 128

D. 256

331. What is the binary equivalent of the dotted-decimal subnet mask 255.255.255.252?

A. 11111111 11111111 11111111 11111100

B. 11111111 11111111 11111111 11111000

C. 11111111 11111111 11111111 11111110

D. 11111111 11111111 11111111 11111100

332. How many bits are used for the host part in a /20 prefix mask?

A. 12

B. 16

C. 20

D. 32

333. Which prefix mask has 26 binary 1s?

A. /24

B. /25

C. /26

D. /27

334. What is the dotted-decimal equivalent of the binary mask 11111111 11111111 11111100 00000000?

A. 255.255.255.0

B. 255.255.252.0

C. 255.255.254.0

D. 255.255.255.192

335. What is the total number of hosts possible in a subnet with mask 255.255.255.0?

A. 254

B. 256

C. 512

D. 1024

336. Which of the following is a valid /18 subnet mask in dotted-decimal notation?

A. 255.255.255.128

B. 255.255.192.0

C. 255.255.255.0

D. 255.255.255.240

337. Which prefix mask corresponds to the dotted-decimal subnet mask 255.255.255.240?

A. /24

B. /26

C. /28

D. /30

338. What type of network topology is commonly used in Ethernet LANs, where all devices are connected to a central hub or switch?
A. Mesh network
B. Bus network
C. Ring network
D. Star network

339. What is a characteristic feature of a full mesh network topology?
A. Centralized control
B. Redundant paths between nodes
C. Single point of failure
D. Limited scalability

340. What is the decimal equivalent of the binary mask 11111111 11111111 11111000 00000000?
A. 255.255.255.0
B. 255.255.248.0
C. 255.255.252.0
D. 255.255.254.0

341. What is the prefix length for a subnet mask of 255.255.255.252?
A. /28
B. /30
C. /31
D. /32

342. What is the dotted-decimal equivalent of the prefix mask /16?
A. 255.255.0.0
B. 255.255.255.0
C. 255.255.255.128
D. 255.255.255.192

343. How many binary 1s are there in the subnet mask 255.255.255.128?
A. 24

B. 25
C. 26
D. 27

344. What is the binary equivalent of the prefix mask /22?
A. 11111111 11111111 11111000 00000000
B. 11111111 11111111 11111100 00000000
C. 11111111 11111111 11111110 00000000
D. 11111111 11111111 11111111 00000000

345. How many hosts can be supported in a subnet with a /30 prefix mask?
A. 2
B. 4
C. 6
D. 8

346. Which of the following is a valid subnet mask for a /31 prefix?
A. 255.255.255.252
B. 255.255.255.254
C. 255.255.255.255
D. 255.255.255.248

347. What is the prefix mask for 255.255.255.128?
A. /24
B. /25
C. /26
D. /27

348. What is the binary equivalent of the decimal mask 255.255.254.0?
A. 11111111 11111111 11111110 00000000
B. 11111111 11111111 11111111 00000000
C. 11111111 11111111 11111100 00000000
D. 11111111 11111111 11111000 00000000

349. What is the dotted-decimal equivalent of the binary mask 11111111 11111111 11111111 11111110?

A. 255.255.255.252
B. 255.255.255.254
C. 255.255.255.255
D. 255.255.255.248

350. How many binary os are there in the subnet mask 255.255.252.0?
A. 10
B. 12
C. 14
D. 16

351. Which command is used to verify the reachability of an IPv6 address from a Cisco router?
A. ping ipv6
B. ping6
C. ping
D. ipv6 ping

352. In EIGRP, what is the purpose of the "feasible successor"?
A. It is the primary route used for forwarding packets.
B. It is a backup route stored in the topology table.
C. It is the default route used by EIGRP.
D. It is the route with the lowest administrative distance.

353. Which statement is true regarding the default gateway for hosts in a VLAN?
A. Each host can have multiple default gateways.
B. The default gateway must reside within the same VLAN as the hosts.
C. Hosts do not require a default gateway if they are in a VLAN.
D. The default gateway is only needed for inter-VLAN routing.

354. What does the "router-id" command do in the OSPF configuration?
A. It assigns an IP address to an OSPF router.
B. It uniquely identifies the OSPF process on the router.
C. It sets the router's priority in the OSPF domain.
D. It configures the OSPF area ID for the router.

355. Which command configures an IPv6 address on a router interface?
A. ipv6 address
B. ip address ipv6
C. set ipv6 address
D. configure ipv6 address

356. Which protocol is used by IPv6 to replace ARP in IPv4 networks?
A. NDP
B. ICMPv6
C. DHCPv6
D. RIPng

357. What is the main purpose of the Spanning Tree Protocol (STP)?
A. To increase the speed of the network.
B. To provide multiple paths for redundancy.
C. To prevent network loops.
D. To dynamically assign IP addresses.

358. Which command is used to configure an ACL to permit only HTTP traffic from a specific host?
A. access-list 100 permit tcp host 192.168.1.1 eq 80
B. access-list 100 permit ip any eq 80
C. access-list 100 permit tcp 192.168.1.1 0.0.0.0 eq 80
D. access-list 100 permit tcp any host 192.168.1.1 eq 80

359. What is the purpose of the no ip domain-lookup command?
A. To disable DNS lookup when a command is mistyped.
B. To prevent the router from acting as a DNS server.
C. To remove the domain name from the configuration.
D. To disable IP address resolution.

360. Which multicast address is used by OSPF for all OSPF routers?
A. 224.0.0.5
B. 224.0.0.6
C. 224.0.0.9

D. 224.0.0.10

361. Which command is used to set the bandwidth on a serial interface?
A. bandwidth
B. set bandwidth
C. speed
D. interface bandwidth

362. What is the function of the ip sla command?
A. To configure a Service Level Agreement (SLA) monitoring operation.
B. To configure an IP address on a router.
C. To set the speed of an interface.
D. To define the IP route for a specific SLA.

363. Which command is used to verify the NAT translations on a router?
A. show ip nat translations
B. show nat translations
C. show ip nat
D. show ip nat stats

364. What is the default hold time for EIGRP hello packets?
A. 5 seconds
B. 10 seconds
C. 15 seconds
D. 60 seconds

365. Which protocol uses 224.0.0.9 as a multicast address?
A. OSPF
B. EIGRP
C. RIP
D. BGP

366. What is the main function of HSRP?
A. To provide redundancy for default gateways
B. To route multicast traffic
C. To assign IP addresses dynamically

D. To encrypt data traffic

367. Which command is used to configure a static route in a Cisco router?
A. ip route
B. route static
C. set route
D. ip routing

368. Which layer of the OSI model does the MAC address belong to?
A. Network layer
B. Data Link layer
C. Physical layer
D. Transport layer

369. Which command displays the IP routing table on a Cisco router?
A. show ip route
B. show route
C. display ip routing
D. ip show route

370. Which protocol does PPP use to provide authentication?
A. PAP and CHAP
B. EAP
C. 802.1X
D. RADIUS

371. Which command would you use to enable IPv6 routing on a Cisco router?
A. ipv6 routing
B. ipv6 enable
C. ipv6 unicast-routing
D. ipv6 route

372. What is the purpose of the no shutdown command on a Cisco router interface?
A. To disable the interface

B. To enable the interface

C. To reset the interface

D. To configure the interface IP address

373. Which command is used to configure a router as a DHCP server?

A. ip dhcp pool

B. dhcp server

C. set dhcp pool

D. configure dhcp

374. What is the primary function of NAT?

A. To encrypt data traffic

B. To translate private IP addresses to public IP addresses

C. To provide redundancy

D. To dynamically assign IP addresses

375. Which command is used to view the status of a specific interface on a Cisco router?

A. show interfaces

B. show ip interface brief

C. show interface status

D. display interface

376. What does the acronym PoE stand for in networking?

A. Protocol over Ethernet

B. Power over Ethernet

C. Packet over Ethernet

D. Port over Ethernet

377. Which command enables IPv4 forwarding on a Cisco router?

A. ip routing

B. ipv4 enable

C. ip forward

D. enable routing

378. Which command would you use to apply an access list to a router interface?
A. ip access-group
B. access-list apply
C. set access-list
D. access-group

379. What is the default VLAN on Cisco switches?
A. VLAN 1
B. VLAN 100
C. VLAN 1000
D. VLAN 0

380. Which protocol uses TCP port 179 for communication?
A. OSPF
B. EIGRP
C. BGP
D. RIP

381. Which of the following OSPF area types does not accept summary LSAs (Type 3) from other areas?
A. Stub Area
B. Totally Stubby Area
C. Not-So-Stubby Area (NSSA)
D. Backbone Area

382. What is the default administrative distance of OSPF routes?
A. 90
B. 110
C. 120
D. 115

383. Which command can be used to redistribute OSPF routes into EIGRP with a metric of 1000?
A. redistribute ospf 1 metric 1000
B. redistribute ospf 1 metric 1000 under eigrp

C. redistribute ospf 1 metric 1000 under ospf

D. redistribute ospf 1 metric-type 1 metric 1000

384. Which IPv6 address type is equivalent to a private IPv4 address in terms of scope and usage?

A. Global Unicast

B. Link-Local

C. Unique Local

D. Multicast

385. Which command is used to configure an EtherChannel with LACP on a Cisco switch?

A. channel-group 1 mode active

B. port-channel 1 mode passive

C. etherchannel 1 mode on

D. interface port-channel 1 mode active

386. What is the purpose of the BGP next-hop-self command?

A. To set the next hop for iBGP routes to the IP address of the local router

B. To set the next hop for eBGP routes to the IP address of the remote router

C. To configure the router as the default gateway for BGP

D. To reset the BGP session

387. Which protocol is used to synchronize time across network devices?

A. NTP

B. SNMP

C. FTP

D. TFTP

388. What is the main advantage of using IPv6 over IPv4 in terms of address configuration?

A. Larger address space

B. No need for NAT

C. Simplified header format

D. Stateless address autoconfiguration (SLAAC)

389. Which command is used to verify the OSPF neighbor relationships on a Cisco router?
A. show ip ospf neighbors
B. show ospf neighbors
C. show ip ospf neighbor
D. show ip ospf interface

390. Which technology allows multiple VLANs to be configured on a single switchport?
A. Access port
B. Trunking
C. EtherChannel
D. Port Security

391. Which command is used to configure a router to send all log messages to a syslog server?
A. logging trap
B. logging host
C. logging console
D. logging buffer

392. What is the purpose of the ip tcp adjust-mss command?
A. To set the maximum segment size for TCP packets
B. To configure the maximum frame size on an interface
C. To adjust the MTU for IP packets
D. To change the default TCP window size

393. Which routing protocol uses the Diffusing Update Algorithm (DUAL) to ensure loop-free and reliable routes?
A. OSPF
B. EIGRP
C. RIP
D. BGP

394. Which command displays detailed information about the OSPF LSAs in the OSPF database?
A. show ip ospf lsa
B. show ip ospf database
C. show ip ospf summary
D. show ip ospf topology

395. Which command is used to configure a router to summarize OSPF routes?
A. area range
B. area range summary
C. summary-address
D. summary-range

396. Which technology can be used to segment a network into multiple broadcast domains without using multiple physical switches?
A. VLANs
B. Trunking
C. Port Mirroring
D. STP

397. What is the main benefit of using route summarization in OSPF?
A. Reduced size of the routing table
B. Faster convergence times
C. Improved security
D. Increased bandwidth

398. Which feature of HSRP ensures that a single IP address is used for the virtual router?
A. Virtual IP
B. Standby IP
C. Shared IP
D. Floating IP

399. Which command is used to enable BGP on a router and specify the local AS number?

A. router bgp <AS-number>

B. enable bgp <AS-number>

C. bgp router <AS-number>

D. set bgp <AS-number>

400. Which command displays the current spanning-tree configuration for a specific VLAN on a Cisco switch?

A. show spanning-tree vlan <vlan-id>

B. show spanning-tree configuration

C. show vlan spanning-tree

D. display spanning-tree vlan

Answer

1. **Answer:** D) Option B and C

Explanation: UDP and TCP are both protocols that operate at the transport layer in the TCP/IP model.

2. **Answer:** A) Ethernet

Explanation: Ethernet and PPP (Point-to-Point Protocol) are data-link layer protocols in the TCP/IP model.

3. **Answer:** B) Adjacent-layer interaction

Explanation: HTTP (an application layer protocol) asks TCP (a transport layer protocol) to send data, demonstrating adjacent-layer interaction.

4. **Answer:** B) Same-layer interaction

Explanation: This is an example of same-layer interaction where TCP on both sending and receiving computers interact.

5. **Answer:** A) Data encapsulation

Explanation: This process involves adding headers and trailers at each layer, known as data encapsulation.

6. **Answer:** D) Frame

Explanation: The term "frame" is used specifically at the data-link layer to describe the data encapsulated with headers and trailers.

7. **Answer:** B) Layer 2 PDU

Explanation: In the OSI model, a Layer 2 Protocol Data Unit (PDU) is also known as a frame.

8. **Answer:** D) All of the above

Explanation: A networking model defines logical rules for communication, physical requirements, and how different parts of the network should work together.

9. **Answer:** C) TCP/IP

Explanation: TCP/IP is ubiquitous in modern networking, serving as the foundational protocol suite for the vast majority of Internet and corporate networks worldwide due to its robustness, scalability, and compatibility across diverse hardware and software platforms.

10. **Answer:** B) Networking blueprint

Explanation: A networking model is also referred to as a networking blueprint, as it serves as a detailed plan for network design and implementation.

11. **Answer:** B) ISO

Explanation: The International Organization for Standardization (ISO) started the task of creating the OSI networking model.

12. **Answer:** B) To standardize data networking protocols for global communication

Explanation: The main goal of the OSI model was to standardize data networking protocols to allow communication among all computers globally.

13. Answer: C) TCP/IP

Explanation: The TCP/IP model emerged as a competing open networking model from a U.S. Department of Defense contract.

14. Answer: B) TCP/IP

Explanation: By the end of the 1990s, TCP/IP had become the common choice for networking models.

15. Answer: B) Requests For Comments (RFCs)

Explanation: TCP/IP uses documents called Requests For Comments (RFCs) to define protocols.

16. Answer: D) Physical

Explanation: The Physical layer of the TCP/IP model focuses on how to transmit bits over each link.

17. Answer: D) HTTP

Explanation: HTTP (Hypertext Transfer Protocol) indeed operates at the Application layer of the TCP/IP networking model. It facilitates communication between web browsers and servers, enabling the retrieval and display of web pages and other resources over the internet.

18. Answer: C) Network

Explanation: The Network layer is responsible for delivering data over the entire path from the original sending computer to the final destination computer.

19. Answer: A) How web browsers can pull the contents of a web page from a web server

Explanation: The HTTP protocol defines how web browsers can pull the contents of a web page from a web server.

20. **Answer:** C) Error recovery

Explanation: The TCP transport layer protocol provides error recovery services to the application layer.

21. **Answer:** C) Network Layer

Explanation: The Internet Protocol (IP) is part of the Network Layer in the TCP/IP model.

22. **Answer:** B) Addressing and routing

Explanation: The main function of IP is to provide addressing and routing to ensure data packets reach their correct destinations.

23. **Answer:** B) Router

Explanation: Routers are responsible for forwarding packets of data to the correct destinations in a TCP/IP network.

24. **Answer:** A) Any device connected to a TCP/IP network

Explanation: The term 'IP host' refers to any device with an IP address that connects to a TCP/IP network.

25. **Answer:** C) The postal service infrastructure

Explanation: The lower layers of the TCP/IP model act like the postal service infrastructure, handling the delivery of data.

26. **Answer:** C) Dotted-decimal notation

Explanation: The IP address format used in the example is dotted-decimal notation (e.g., 1.1.1.1).

27. **Answer:** C) Forwards the packet based on the destination IP address

Explanation: Routers forward packets by examining the destination IP address and using their routing tables to decide where to send the packet next.

28. **Answer:** C) IP

Explanation: IP is part of the Network Layer, not the Transport Layer. The Transport Layer includes TCP and UDP.

29. **Answer:** B) Chooses to send the packet to a nearby router

Explanation: Larry's IP process sends the packet to a nearby router, expecting it to forward the packet correctly.

30. **Answer:** A) Defines how data is transmitted across the physical network

Explanation: The data-link layer defines the protocols and hardware required to deliver data across the physical network.

31. **Answer:** D) Application layer

Explanation: The application layer is responsible for creating and encapsulating the application data with any required headers.

32. **Answer:** B) Application, Transport, Network, Data-link, Physical

Explanation: The correct order of encapsulation in the TCP/IP model starts from the application layer and goes down to the physical layer.

33. Answer: C) Segment

Explanation: The term "segment" is used to refer to a message at the transport layer in the TCP/IP model.

34. Answer: D) Step 5

Explanation: Step 5 in the TCP/IP encapsulation process involves the physical transmission of data as bits.

35. Answer: B) Layer 3

Explanation: In the OSI (Open Systems Interconnection) model, the network layer corresponds to Layer 3. This layer is responsible for routing packets across different networks, addressing, and logical network topology. It ensures that data packets are routed efficiently from the source to the destination across interconnected networks. Examples of protocols operating at this layer include IP (Internet Protocol) and ICMP (Internet Control Message Protocol).

36. Answer: C) Logical Addressing

Explanation: Logical addressing is a function of the network layer, not the data-link layer.

37. Answer: C) IP packets

Explanation: The Ethernet link layer encapsulates the IP packets inside both a header and a trailer.

38. Answer: D) Protocol Data Unit (PDU)

Explanation: In the OSI model, the term PDU is used generically to refer to messages, and at the network layer, it is called a Layer 3 PDU (L3PDU).

39. **Answer:** C) To provide error detection and correction

Explanation: The trailer in the data-link layer typically contains error detection and correction information.

40. **Answer:** D) Physical layer

Explanation: The physical layer in the TCP/IP model has functions equivalent to those of the physical layer in the OSI model.

41. **Answer:** C) 1000BASE-T

Explanation: 1000BASE-T is the Ethernet standard that defines Gigabit Ethernet over UTP (Unshielded Twisted Pair) cabling.

42. **Answer:** A) Only the devices that use cables are using Ethernet.

Explanation: Ethernet refers to wired LAN technology using cables, while wireless devices use wireless LAN technology.

43. **Answer:** B) Pins 1 and 2 on one end of the cable connect to pins 3 and 6 on the other end of the cable.

Explanation: For Ethernet crossover cables, pins 1 and 2 on one end connect to pins 3 and 6 on the other end, allowing direct device-to-device connections.

44. **Answer:** B) ARP

Explanation:

ARP (Address Resolution Protocol) is used to map IP addresses to MAC addresses. When a device wants to communicate with another device on the same local network, it uses ARP to find the MAC address associated with the IP address of the destination device.

45. **Answer:** B) To extend the link beyond 100 meters while keeping initial costs as low as possible.

Explanation: Multimode fiber is often chosen to extend the link beyond 100 meters while managing costs, though it doesn't achieve the longest possible distances compared to single-mode fiber.

46. **Answer:** B) Collisions can happen, but the algorithm defines how the computers should notice a collision and how to recover.

Explanation: The CSMA/CD algorithm allows for collisions and defines a method for detecting and recovering from them.

47. **Answer:** C) It resides in the Ethernet trailer, not the Ethernet header.

Explanation: The Ethernet FCS (Frame Check Sequence) field is located in the Ethernet trailer and is used for error detection, not recovery.

48. **Answer:** C) crypto key generate rsa

Explanation: The crypto key generate rsa command generates RSA key pairs required for SSH, enabling secure remote management of the switch.

49. **Answer:** B) To prevent unauthorized DHCP servers from providing IP addresses.

Explanation: DHCP snooping is a security feature that acts as a firewall between untrusted hosts and trusted DHCP servers, preventing unauthorized (rogue) DHCP servers from assigning IP addresses to devices.

50. **Answer:** C) Wireless router

Explanation: SOHO networks often use a single "wireless router" device that combines the functionality of a router and an Ethernet switch.

51. Answer: B) 802.3

Explanation: All Ethernet standards come from the IEEE and include the number 802.3 as the beginning part of the standard name.

52. Answer: B) Copper, 100 m

Explanation: 1000BASE-T, also known as Gigabit Ethernet, uses copper cabling with a maximum length of 100 meters.

53. Answer: C) 10BASE-T Encoding

Explanation: 10BASE-T uses an encoding scheme where a binary 0 is encoded as a transition from higher voltage to lower voltage during the middle of a 1/10,000,000th-of-a-second interval.

54. Answer: A) 100 m

Explanation: Yes, that's correct. The maximum length for a 10BASE-T Ethernet cable, which is a type of twisted pair Ethernet cable used in traditional Ethernet networks, is indeed 100 meters. This limitation is due to signal attenuation and timing constraints within the Ethernet protocol. Exceeding this cable length can lead to issues such as data loss, signal degradation, and unreliable network connections. Therefore, it's important to adhere to this maximum length when deploying Ethernet networks to ensure optimal performance and reliability.

55. Answer: B) Longer cabling distances

Explanation: Fiber-optic cabling, although more expensive, typically allows Ethernet nodes to have longer cabling distances between them compared to UTP cabling.

56. Answer: B) 1000BASE-LX

Explanation: 1000BASE-LX is the informal IEEE standard name for Gigabit Ethernet using fiber cabling with a maximum length of 5000 meters.

57. **Answer:** B) To reduce electromagnetic interference (EMI)

Explanation: Twisting the wire pairs together helps cancel out most of the EMI, including crosstalk.

58. **Answer:** B) RJ-45

Explanation: Many Ethernet UTP (Unshielded Twisted Pair) cables indeed utilize an RJ-45 connector on both ends, facilitating standardized connectivity across Ethernet networks. This connector type ensures compatibility with Ethernet devices, providing a reliable and widely accepted method for network connections.

59. **Answer:** C) 400 Gbps

Explanation: Ethernet standards now define speeds up to 400 gigabits per second (Gbps).

60. **Answer:** C) Sending Ethernet frames from source to destination

Explanation: The Ethernet data-link layer protocols focus on sending an Ethernet frame from the source to the destination Ethernet node.

61. **Answer:** C) SFP+

Explanation*: SFP+ is the transceiver used on 10-Gbps interfaces, as noted in the text.

62. **Answer:** B) SFP+ supports higher speeds

Explanation: The main difference between SFP (Small Form-factor Pluggable) and SFP+ (Enhanced Small Form-factor Pluggable) modules is the data rate they support. SFP modules typically support speeds up to 1 Gbps, while SFP+ modules support higher speeds, up to 10 Gbps. This allows SFP+ to be used in applications requiring higher bandwidth compared to SFP.

63. Answer: A) Pins 1 and 2

Explanation: PC NIC transmitters use the pair connected to pins 1 and 2 in 10BASE-T and 100BASE-T networks.

64. Answer: B) Crossover cable

Explanation: A crossover cable is required because both switches transmit on the same pin pairs.

65. Answer: C) 4

Explanation: Yes, that's correct. 1000BASE-T, which is also known as Gigabit Ethernet, utilizes all four wire pairs (eight wires total) within a Category 5e (or higher) twisted-pair cable. This configuration allows for full-duplex communication at gigabit speeds over Ethernet networks. Each pair is used for both transmitting and receiving data, ensuring high-speed and efficient data transfer.

66. Answer: B) It can reach greater distances

Explanation: Fiber cabling is used to reach greater distances, among other reasons.

67. Answer: B) Straight-through cable pinout

Explanation: A straight-through cable pinout is used when connecting a PC to a switch in a 10BASE-T or 100BASE-T network.

68. Answer: C) Auto-mdix

Explanation: Cisco switches have the auto-mdix feature, which adjusts for incorrect cable types.

69. Answer: D) Switches

Explanation: In 10BASE-T and 100BASE-T Ethernet networks, switches and other networking equipment typically transmit data on pins 3 and 6 of the RJ-45 connector. These pins correspond to the orange wire pair (pair 2) in a standard Ethernet cable. The other pair used for transmission is the green wire pair (pair 3), which corresponds to pins 1 and 2. This arrangement ensures proper communication between devices in the network, adhering to the Ethernet wiring standards.

70. Answer: C) Pins 4 and 5, and 7 and 8

Explanation: The Gigabit Ethernet crossover cable uses additional pairs at pins 4 and 5, and 7 and 8, which are not used in 10BASE-T or 100BASE-T crossover cables.

71. Answer: C) Glass

Explanation: Fiber-optic cabling uses glass, specifically fiberglass, as the medium through which light passes to encode data.

72. Answer: B) To reflect light into the core

Explanation: The cladding in a fiber-optic cable reflects light into the core, allowing the light to travel through the core efficiently.

73. Answer: B) Multimode fiber

Explanation: Multimode fiber allows for multiple angles (modes) of light waves to enter the core, enabling data transmission.

74. Answer: B) Laser-based transmitter

Explanation: Single-mode fiber uses a laser-based transmitter to send light at a single angle through its smaller-diameter core.

75. Answer: C) 10km

Explanation: The standard for 10GBASE-LR over single-mode fiber allows for a maximum distance of up to 10km without repeaters.

76. Answer: A) UTP

Explanation: UTP (Unshielded Twisted Pair) cabling is more susceptible to electromagnetic interference (EMI) compared to fiber-optic cables.

77. Answer: C) Single-mode fiber

Explanation: Single-mode fiber allows for distances into the tens of kilometers, making it suitable for long-distance data transmission.

78. Answer: C) Higher

Explanation: The relative cost of switch ports for single-mode fiber is higher compared to UTP due to the more expensive hardware required.

79. Answer: C) No emissions that can be copied

Explanation: Fiber-optic cables do not emit signals that can be intercepted, making them more secure for highly sensitive networks.

80. Answer: A) Small Form-factor Pluggable

Explanation: SFP stands for Small Form-factor Pluggable, which refers to a type of module used in networking hardware for fiber-optic connections.

81. Answer: B) 6 bytes

 Explanation: Ethernet addresses, also called MAC addresses, are 6-byte-long (48-bit-long) binary numbers.

82. Answer: B) IEEE

 Explanation: Before a manufacturer can build Ethernet products, it must ask the IEEE to assign a manufacturer a universally unique 3-byte code called the organizationally unique identifier (OUI).

83. Answer: B) Unicast address

 Explanation:

A unicast address is a MAC address that uniquely identifies a single LAN interface on a network. It ensures that frames are delivered to a specific device. Unlike broadcast addresses (which are intended for all devices on the network) and multicast addresses (which are intended for a group of devices), a unicast address is used for one-to-one communication.

84. Answer: B) FFFF.FFFF.FFFF

 Explanation: Frames sent to the broadcast address (FFFF.FFFF.FFFF) should be delivered to all devices on the Ethernet LAN.

85. Answer: C) Type Field

 Explanation: The Ethernet Type field, or EtherType, identifies the type of network layer (Layer 3) packet that sits inside the Ethernet frame.

86. Answer: A) Error detection

 Explanation: The FCS field gives the receiving node a way to compare results with the sender, to discover whether errors occurred in the frame.

87. **Answer:** B) The frame is discarded

Explanation: If the results of the FCS check do not match, an error occurs, and the receiver discards the frame.

88. **Answer:** C) Universal address

Explanation: The IEEE uses the term universal address to emphasize the fact that the address assigned to a NIC by a manufacturer should be unique among all MAC addresses in the universe.

89. **Answer:** D) Group addresses

Explanation: Group addresses identify more than one LAN interface card, and frames sent to a group address might be delivered to a small set of devices on the LAN or even to all devices on the LAN.

90. **Answer:** C) IP address

Explanation: Ethernet addresses go by many names including LAN address, Ethernet address, hardware address, burned-in address, physical address, universal address, or MAC address, but not IP address.

91. **Answer:** B) The device does not have to wait before sending; it can send and receive at the same time.

Explanation: Full duplex allows devices to send and receive data simultaneously without waiting, unlike half duplex.

92. **Answer:** B) The device must wait to send if it is currently receiving a frame.

Explanation: Half duplex requires devices to wait before sending if they are currently receiving data to prevent collisions.

93. **Answer:** C) LAN hub

Explanation: Before Ethernet switches, LAN hubs were used to connect multiple PCs but operated with different forwarding rules.

94. **Answer:** C) They repeat incoming electrical signals out of all other ports.

Explanation: LAN hubs operate at Layer 1 and repeat electrical signals received on one port to all other ports.

95. **Answer:** C) Because hubs repeat all received electrical signals, even if multiple are received at the same time.

Explanation: This behavior causes signal collisions when multiple devices send data simultaneously.

96. **Answer:** A) Carrier Sense Multiple Access with Collision Detection

Explanation: CSMA/CD is an algorithm used to manage data transmission and detect collisions in Ethernet networks.

97. **Answer:** C) Each link works independently of the others.

Explanation: Ethernet point-to-point links, especially with switches, allow full duplex communication, making each link independent.

98. **Answer:** B) When connected to a LAN hub.

Explanation: Devices connected to LAN hubs should use half duplex to prevent collisions, as hubs do not manage data transmissions.

99. **Answer:** C) The signals collide and become garbled.

Explanation: In a network using a LAN hub, simultaneous transmissions cause signal collisions, making the signals unreadable.

100. **Answer:** B) Designs that use hubs, require CSMA/CD, and share the bandwidth.

Explanation: Ethernet-shared media involves networks with hubs where devices share bandwidth and use CSMA/CD to manage transmissions.

101. **Answer:** B) enable secret love

Explanation: The command `enable secret love` sets the enable secret password to "love" on a Cisco switch.

102. **Answer:** B) line console 0

Explanation: The command `line console 0` is used to enter console configuration mode on a Cisco switch.

103. **Answer:** C) faith

Explanation: In networking configurations, setting "faith" as the password for the console line typically grants access to configure and manage network devices through their console ports. This security measure helps ensure only authorized personnel can make changes to network settings directly from the device itself.

104. **Answer:** D) line vty 0 15 password hope login

Explanation: The command `line vty 0 15 password hope login` allows Telnet users to log in with the password "hope."

105. **Answer:** D) 16

Explanation: In networking, configuring "line vty 0 15" on a switch sets up 16 virtual terminal lines (vty lines), allowing simultaneous remote access via Telnet or SSH to manage the switch. This setup provides flexibility for multiple administrators to securely access and configure the switch remotely.

106. **Answer:** B) login local

Explanation: The command `login local` configures the switch to prompt for both username and password for Telnet users.

107. **Answer:** A) no password

Explanation: The command `no password` removes any existing simple shared passwords for good housekeeping of the configuration file.

108. **Answer:** B) To generate SSH encryption keys

Explanation: The command `crypto key generate rsa` is used to generate SSH encryption keys.

109. **Answer:** A) transport input all

Explanation: The command transport input all on vty lines allows remote access using all available protocols, including SSH and Telnet, unless specifically restricted. This flexibility enables administrators to choose between secure (SSH) and less secure (Telnet) access methods based on their security requirements.

110. **Answer:** C) ip default-gateway

Explanation: The command `ip default-gateway` is used to configure the default gateway on a Cisco switch.

111. Answer: B) Dividing a large network into smaller, more manageable subnets

Explanation: Subnetting divides a large network into smaller, more manageable subnets for efficiency and better management.

112. Answer: B) 172.16.0.0 to 172.16.255.255

Explanation: A Class B network address for 172.16.0.0 includes all addresses from 172.16.0.0 to 172.16.255.255.

113. Answer: C) To divide a large network into smaller, more efficient subnets

Explanation: The primary purpose of subnetting in IP networking is to divide a large network into smaller, more manageable subnets. This segmentation allows for more efficient use of IP addresses by reducing wastage and helps to isolate network segments to improve overall performance and manageability. By breaking down a large network into smaller subnets, it also helps in reducing broadcast traffic, improving network security by limiting access to certain subnets, and simplifying fault isolation. Subnetting does not increase the total number of available IP addresses, but rather optimizes their allocation and use within the network.

114. Answer: B) Subdivided network

Explanation: The term "subnet" stands for a subdivision of a larger network into smaller, logical segments. It allows for efficient management of network resources and enhances security by isolating groups of devices within a network.

115. Answer: B) It allows for more efficient use of IP addresses

Explanation: Subnetting helps in network design by allowing for more efficient use of IP addresses.

116. **Answer:** C) Both inbound and outbound

 Explanation: An ACL can be applied to an interface in both the inbound and outbound directions.

117. **Answer:** B) Hosts that are not separated by a router

 Explanation: Hosts that should be grouped into a subnet are those not separated by a router.

118. **Answer:** C) 7

 Explanation: An internetwork with four VLANs and three point-to-point serial links requires seven subnets.

119. **Answer:** B) To waste fewer IP addresses

 Explanation: Using different subnet sizes in a network design can indeed reduce the waste of IP addresses. By carefully choosing subnet sizes based on the number of devices needed in each subnet, administrators can allocate IP addresses more efficiently. This practice prevents larger subnets from consuming more IP addresses than necessary for smaller segments of the network, thereby optimizing IP address utilization across the network infrastructure.

120. **Answer:** B) configure terminal

 Explanation: To enter configuration mode on a Cisco switch, you use the command configure terminal or its shorthand form `conf t`. This command allows administrators to access the switch's configuration settings where they can modify parameters such as interfaces, VLANs, and security policies. Configuration mode is essential for making changes to the switch's operational behavior and ensuring it aligns with the network's requirements and security standards.

121. **Answer:** B) switchport access vlan

 Explanation: The command switchport access vlan <vlan-id> dynamically creates a VLAN on a Cisco switch if it does not already exist when assigning a port to it. This enables seamless VLAN creation and assignment without the need for prior configuration of the VLAN on the switch.

122. **Answer:** B) VLAN0003

 Explanation: When a switch dynamically creates VLAN 3, the default name assigned to it by the switch is "VLAN0003." This naming convention follows the format of appending the VLAN number with leading zeros to ensure consistency in VLAN naming across the switch's configuration.

123. **Answer:** A) To advertise VLAN configurations to other switches

 Explanation: The purpose of the VLAN Trunking Protocol (VTP) is to advertise VLAN configurations to other switches.

124. **Answer:** C) Transparent

 Explanation: In VTP (VLAN Trunking Protocol), setting a switch to transparent mode indeed disables VTP functions on that switch. In this mode, the switch does not synchronize VLAN information with other switches nor does it advertise or learn VLAN information through VTP advertisements. Transparent mode allows VLANs to be configured locally on the switch without affecting the VTP domain or version. Therefore, any VLAN changes made on a switch in transparent mode do not propagate to other switches in the VTP domain.

125. **Answer:** D) vtp mode off

 Explanation: This command is entered in global configuration mode and stops the switch from sending or receiving VTP advertisements, effectively disabling VTP operation across the switch.

126. Answer: B) show vtp status

 Explanation: This command displays information about the current VTP mode (client, server, transparent), the VTP domain name, and the revision number. It provides an overview of the VTP configuration and operational status of the switch.

127. Answer: B) 802.1Q

 Explanation: Most modern Cisco switches support 802.1Q trunking, which is a standard VLAN trunking protocol used to carry traffic for multiple VLANs over a single physical link between switches or between a switch and a router. It allows for efficient segregation and management of network traffic by tagging Ethernet frames with VLAN identifiers.

128. Answer: A) switchport mode access

 Explanation: When configured with this command, the switch port will not participate in VLAN trunking negotiations and will only carry traffic for a single VLAN, specified by the switchport access vlan command. This is typically used when connecting end devices like computers or printers that are not capable of understanding VLAN tagging.

129. Answer: B) switchport mode trunk

 Explanation: When configured with this command, the switch port will actively negotiate to become a trunk port and will carry traffic for multiple VLANs. Trunk ports are used to interconnect switches or to connect to devices that support and require VLAN tagging, such as other switches, routers, or servers configured with VLANs.

130. Answer: B) dynamic auto

 Explanation: Dynamic auto means the switch will passively negotiate to become a trunk link if the neighboring switch initiates trunking. If no initiation occurs, it remains a non-trunking access link.

131. **Answer:** C) switchport mode dynamic desirable

 Explanation: This command configures the switch port to actively attempt to negotiate a trunk link with the connected device using Dynamic Trunking Protocol (DTP).

132. **Answer:** D) dynamic auto

 Explanation: In this mode, the switch port will passively wait to negotiate a trunk link with another device that is actively attempting to establish a trunk.

133. **Answer:** C) switchport nonegotiate

 Explanation: When configured with this command, the switch port will not send DTP negotiation frames and will not attempt to negotiate a trunk link with connected devices.

134. **Answer:** B) To display trunk information on operational trunk ports

 Explanation: The 'show interfaces trunk' command displays trunk information on operational trunk ports.

135. **Answer:** C) Access and trunk

 Explanation: Configuring one end of an Ethernet link as 'access' and the other end as 'trunk' should be avoided because it can lead to mismatched VLAN configurations and operational issues. It's best to maintain consistency in VLAN configuration on both ends of a link to ensure proper communication and avoid unintended network problems.

136. **Answer:** A) VLAN 1

Explanation: In Cisco networking, VLAN 1 is designated as the default native VLAN. This means untagged traffic on a trunk port will be associated with VLAN 1 unless explicitly configured otherwise.

137. **Answer:** B) Cause VLAN configuration changes across the network

Explanation: Changing VTP settings on a switch connected to the production network can cause VLAN configuration changes across the network.

138. **Answer:** A) No output

Explanation: If no interfaces are operationally trunking, the 'show interfaces trunk' command produces no output.

139. **Answer:** A) switchport mode access

Explanation: The command "switchport mode access" ensures that a switch port is configured to operate strictly as an access port, preventing it from participating in trunk negotiations or sending trunking DTP messages. This configuration is essential for connecting end devices or devices that do not support trunking.

140. **Answer:** C) show vlan brief

Explanation: The command "show vlan" is used on Cisco switches to display the VLAN configuration, including details such as VLAN IDs, names, and port assignments. It provides an overview of how VLANs are configured across the switch's ports and their associated VLAN membership.

141. **Answer:** A) Creates the VLAN

Explanation: The 'switchport access vlan' command assigns an access VLAN to a switch port and does not create the VLAN if it does not already exist in the VLAN database of the switch. To create a VLAN, you need to use the 'vlan' command in global configuration mode to define the VLAN and then assign it to the switch port using 'switchport access vlan' in interface configuration mode.

142. **Answer:** A) Configuring standard and extended-range VLANs

Explanation: In VTP Transparent mode, VLANs can be configured locally on the switch without synchronization to other switches in the network. This mode supports both standard (1-1005) and extended-range (1006-4094) VLANs, offering flexibility in VLAN management.

143. **Answer:** D) Never trunk

Explanation: If both ends of a link are configured with 'switchport mode dynamic auto,' the link will never trunk by default.

144. **Answer:** A) Initiates trunk negotiation

Explanation: The command switchport mode dynamic desirable on a Cisco switch port initiates Dynamic Trunking Protocol (DTP) negotiation. This allows the port to actively try to become a trunk port if the neighboring port supports trunking.

145. **Answer:** A) vlan 10

Explanation: The vlan 10 command in Cisco IOS configures VLAN 10 on a switch. This command is used in global configuration mode to create and configure VLANs on the switch.

146. **Answer:** A) Active

Explanation: In Cisco switches, the default state of a VLAN created automatically is indeed active. This means the VLAN is operational and can forward traffic unless explicitly configured otherwise.

147. Answer: D) switchport mode trunk

Explanation: The command you're looking for is switchport mode dynamic desirable. It configures the switch port to trunk mode and allows negotiation of trunking settings with the connected device.

148. Answer: B) Brief summary of VLANs and their status

Explanation: The 'show vlan brief' command provides a concise overview of all VLANs configured on the switch, including their VLAN IDs, names, and status (active or suspended).

149. Answer: A) Forces the port to become a trunk

Explanation: The command 'switchport mode trunk' explicitly configures the port to operate as a trunk link, regardless of the dynamic negotiation with the neighboring device. This ensures the port will always transmit and receive tagged VLAN traffic.

150. Answer: B) Standard-range VLANs only

Explanation: A switch operating in VTP server or client mode is limited to managing VLANs within the standard range (VLAN IDs 1-1005), excluding extended-range VLANs (VLAN IDs 1006-4094), which are supported only in VTP transparent mode.

151. Answer: B) It cannot configure VLANs

Explanation: In VTP client mode, a switch cannot create or modify VLANs; it can only receive and synchronize VLAN configuration updates from VTP servers. This ensures VLAN consistency across the network while restricting configuration capabilities to VTP servers.

152. Answer: C) Dynamic Trunking Protocol

Explanation: Dynamic Trunking Protocol (DTP) is a Cisco proprietary protocol used to negotiate trunking between switches automatically, simplifying VLAN configuration by dynamically establishing trunk links.

153. **Answer:** C) Negotiate

Explanation: The default mode of a switch that supports both ISL and 802.1Q is to negotiate the trunking protocol.

154. **Answer:** A) switchport mode dynamic desirable

Explanation: This command sets an administrative mode that initiates trunk negotiation and also responds to it.

155. **Answer:** B) The link will trunk

Explanation: The link will trunk if one switch port is set to 'dynamic desirable' and the other to 'dynamic auto'.

156. **Answer:** A) show interfaces switchport

Explanation: The command show interfaces switchport is used to view the operational mode of a switch interface. It provides detailed information about whether the interface is configured as an access port or a trunk port, along with VLAN membership and other switchport-specific settings.

157. **Answer:** A) Disables DTP negotiations

Explanation: The switchport nonegotiate command is used on Cisco switches to disable Dynamic Trunking Protocol (DTP) negotiations on a specific interface. DTP is used by Cisco switches to negotiate whether an interface should operate as an access port or a trunk port dynamically. Setting switchport nonegotiate prevents DTP negotiations and manually configures the interface as either an access port or a trunk port depending on the current configuration.

158. Answer: A) Disables VTP completely

Explanation: Setting vtp mode off disables VLAN Trunking Protocol (VTP) completely on a Cisco switch. VTP is used to manage VLAN configurations across multiple switches in a network. By setting the mode to 'off', the switch does not participate in VTP updates, does not synchronize VLAN configuration changes, and operates independently regarding VLAN management.

159. Answer: C) vtp mode transparent

Explanation: The command to change the VTP mode to transparent on a Cisco switch is vtp mode transparent. This setting ensures that the switch does not participate in VTP domain-wide VLAN management and does not propagate VLAN information to other switches.

160. Answer: C) Initiate and respond to negotiation

Explanation: The switchport mode dynamic desirable command on a Cisco switch enables the interface to actively attempt to negotiate trunking by sending DTP (Dynamic Trunking Protocol) frames and also respond to negotiation requests from the connected device. This mode allows the interface to dynamically become a trunk if the neighboring device is set to auto or desirable mode, promoting trunk formation based on negotiation.

161. Answer: B) switchport mode access

Explanation: The command switchport mode access ensures that a switch port is statically configured as an access port, preventing it from participating in trunk negotiation or forming trunk links with other switches. This configuration is typically used when the port is intended to connect to end devices rather than other switches or network devices requiring trunking capabilities.

Answers

162. Answer: A) VLAN 1

Explanation: In an 802.1Q trunk configuration, VLAN 1 is used as the default VLAN for frames that arrive on the trunk without any VLAN tag. This ensures compatibility and allows untagged frames to be placed into a specific VLAN for communication within the network.

163. Answer: B) switchport mode access

Explanation: The command "switchport mode access" configures a switch port to operate in access mode, where the port can carry traffic for a single VLAN without any VLAN tagging. This is typically used to connect end devices such as computers or printers directly to the switch.

164. Answer: B) VLAN configurations

Explanation: The show vlan command is used on Cisco switches to display detailed information about VLAN configurations, including VLAN IDs, names, interfaces assigned to each VLAN, and their statuses such as active or inactive. This command is essential for network administrators to verify and manage VLAN assignments and configurations within the network infrastructure.

165. Answer: C) May trunk if negotiation is successful

Explanation: If both ends are configured with 'switchport mode dynamic auto,' the link may trunk if the negotiation is successful.

166. Answer: B) The switch does not participate in VTP

Explanation: Configuring 'vtp mode transparent' means the switch does not participate in VTP.

167. Answer: D) switchport nonegotiate

Explanation: This command sets the interface to trunk mode and disables DTP.

168. **Answer:** C) Segment network traffic

Explanation: One of the main purposes of using VLANs is to segment network traffic.

169. **Answer:** B) One must be set to dynamic desirable

Explanation: For two switches to successfully negotiate trunking, one must be set to dynamic desirable.

170. **Answer:** B) To prevent looping frames

Explanation: STP/RSTP was designed specifically to prevent Ethernet frames from looping indefinitely in a network.

171. **Answer:** C) By adding an additional check on each interface

Explanation: STP/RSTP adds an additional check on each interface to decide whether to forward or block traffic.

172. **Answer:** B) It blocks all user traffic and does not send or receive user traffic

Explanation: An interface in a blocking state will not forward or receive user traffic in that VLAN.

173. **Answer:** A) Normal, forwarding and receiving frames

Explanation: Interfaces in the forwarding state act as normal, handling traffic as usual.

174. Answer: B) The indefinite looping of broadcast frames

Explanation: A broadcast storm occurs when broadcast frames loop indefinitely, causing network congestion.

175. Answer: B) MAC table stability

Explanation: MAC table stability is not a problem; looping frames instead cause MAC table instability.

176. Answer: C) Blocking certain switch ports

Explanation: STP/RSTP prevents loops by blocking certain switch ports to break potential loops.

177. Answer: A) Frames loop indefinitely

Explanation: During a broadcast storm, frames loop indefinitely until the loop is broken.

178. Answer: B) The continual updating of MAC address tables with incorrect entries

Explanation: MAC table instability arises when switches constantly update their MAC address tables with incorrect information due to looping frames. This continuous updating leads to network congestion and disrupted communication.

179. Answer: B) To prevent looping frames

Explanation: The primary goal of placing ports in forwarding or blocking states is to prevent looping frames.

180. Answer: B) The process of making switches block or forward on each interface

Explanation: STP convergence refers to the process of determining which ports should block and which should forward.

181. **Answer:** B) A spanning tree of interfaces

Explanation: STP/RSTP creates a spanning tree to manage traffic efficiently and prevent loops.

182. **Answer:** D) Ignore user frames except STP/RSTP messages

Explanation: Interfaces in the blocking state ignore all user frames except for STP/RSTP messages.

183. **Answer:** C) Not using the link between switches for traffic in a VLAN

Explanation: One negative effect of STP is that it might block some redundant links, thus not using them for traffic.

184. **Answer:** B) It does not process any frames except STP/RSTP messages

Explanation: When a port is in the blocking state, it only processes STP/RSTP messages and no other frames.

185. **Answer:** B) Looping Ethernet frames

Explanation: Looping Ethernet frames cause broadcast storms, saturating the network.

186. **Answer:** C) To ensure all devices receive the broadcast

Explanation: Switches flood broadcasts to ensure that all devices in the same VLAN receive the broadcast.

187. **Answer:** C) Floods the frame out all interfaces

Explanation: When a switch receives a frame with an unknown destination MAC, it floods the frame out all interfaces.

188. **Answer:** B) Multiple copies of one frame being delivered to the intended host

Explanation: Looping frames can result in multiple copies of the same frame being delivered to the destination.

189. **Answer:** B) When something changes in the LAN topology

Explanation: STP/RSTP convergence occurs when there is a change in the network topology, requiring a recalculation of states.

190. **Answer:** C) Converges to change state from blocking to forwarding

Explanation: STP (Spanning Tree Protocol) and RSTP (Rapid Spanning Tree Protocol) are network protocols used to prevent loops in Ethernet networks, which can occur during network outages or changes. When a network outage occurs, these protocols undergo a convergence process to reconfigure the network topology and ensure that data frames can continue to be forwarded without causing loops. This convergence process involves changing the state of ports from blocking (where no data is forwarded) to forwarding (where data can be forwarded), thereby restoring network connectivity in a stable manner.

191. **Answer:** B) They connect LANs and implement STP/RSTP

Explanation: In STP/RSTP, switches play the same role as bridges, connecting LANs and preventing loops.

192. **Answer:** B) To prevent loops in Ethernet LANs

Explanation: The primary function of Spanning Tree Protocol (STP) and Rapid Spanning Tree Protocol (RSTP) is to prevent loops in Ethernet LANs.

They achieve this by creating a loop-free logical topology, ensuring reliable and efficient network communication.

193. **Answer:** B) Blocking and discarding frames

Explanation: Interfaces in the blocking state discard frames and do not forward them. They listen for BPDUs to prevent loops but do not participate in frame forwarding.

194. **Answer:** C) It gets continually updated with incorrect entries

Explanation: During a broadcast storm, the MAC address table is continually updated with incorrect entries.

195. **Answer:** B) The source MAC has moved to a different port

Explanation: The switch updates its MAC table, thinking the source MAC has moved to a different port.

196. **Answer:** B) Blocks certain switch ports

Explanation: STP/RSTP prevents network loops by selectively placing certain switch ports into a blocking state. This ensures a single active path between network devices, eliminating the possibility of broadcast storms and MAC table instability.

197. **Answer:** D) Ignore user frames except STP/RSTP messages

Explanation: Blocked interfaces do not forward user frames and ignore all traffic except STP/RSTP messages. This allows the switch to manage network topology changes without causing loops.

198. **Answer:** C) Looping frames causing network congestion

Explanation: Without STP/RSTP, looping frames can create broadcast storms, leading to severe network congestion and instability. This can result in degraded network performance and potential outages.

199. **Answer:** B) Frames being sent to the wrong locations

Explanation: MAC table instability sends frames to incorrect locations, causing network inefficiencies and connectivity issues. This happens when switches constantly update their MAC tables due to looping frames.

200. **Answer:** C) Converges to change state from blocking to forwarding

Explanation: STP/RSTP handles outages by changing the state of ports to activate redundant links, ensuring network continuity. This dynamic adjustment prevents loops and maintains network stability.

201. **Answer:** B) Forward and receive frames as normal

Explanation: Interfaces in the forwarding state operate normally, handling traffic as expected.

202. **Answer:** C) To create a single path to and from each Ethernet link

Explanation: The spanning tree structure ensures a single path for traffic, preventing loops.

203. **Answer:** A) They loop indefinitely

Explanation: During broadcast storms, frames loop indefinitely until the loop is broken.

204. **Answer:** B) spanning-tree vlan 10 root primary

Explanation: The spanning-tree vlan 10 root primary command configures the switch to be the root bridge for VLAN 10 by setting the switch's priority to a value lower than the default, which is likely to be lower than other switches in the network.

205. **Answer:** D) It assigns the 192.168.1.0/24 network to area 0.

 Explanation: The command network 192.168.1.0 0.0.0.255 area 0 tells the OSPF process to include interfaces in the 192.168.1.0/24 network in OSPF area 0.

206. **Answer:** B) To prevent loops in Ethernet LANs

 Explanation: The primary function of STP/RSTP is to prevent loops in Ethernet LANs.

207. **Answer:** B) Blocking and discarding frames

 Explanation: Interfaces in the blocking state discard incoming frames and do not forward them. They only process and respond to STP/RSTP messages to maintain network topology.

208. **Answer:** C) It gets continually updated with incorrect entries

 Explanation: During a broadcast storm, the MAC address table is continually updated with incorrect entries.

209. **Answer:** B) The source MAC has moved to a different port

 Explanation: The switch updates its MAC table, thinking the source MAC has moved to a different port.

210. **Answer:** B) Blocks certain switch ports

 Explanation: STP/RSTP prevents loops by blocking certain switch ports.

211. **Answer:** D) Listen

 Explanation: In the HSRP (Hot Standby Router Protocol) Listen state, a router listens for hello messages from the active and standby routers but does not send periodic hello messages itself. Only the active and standby routers send hello messages.

212. **Answer:** A) It enables classful routing behavior.

 Explanation: The no ip classless command causes the router to use classful routing behavior, meaning it will not forward packets to a default route if the destination is not found in the routing table.

213. **Answer:** A) It creates an SLA operation to send ICMP echo requests to IP 10.1.1.1. **Explanation:** The ip sla 1 command creates an IP SLA operation with ID 1, and the icmp-echo 10.1.1.1 specifies that this operation will send ICMP echo requests (pings) to the IP address 10.1.1.1.

214. **Answer:** B) Broadcast

 Explanation: OSPF elects a Designated Router (DR) and Backup Designated Router (BDR) on broadcast and non-broadcast multi-access (NBMA) networks to minimize the number of adjacencies.

215. **Answer:** D) IP

 Explanation: OSPF (Open Shortest Path First) uses IP protocol number 89 to send link-state updates. It operates directly over IP without using TCP or UDP.

216. **Answer:** C) It negotiates trunking with the other port using DTP.

 Explanation: The switchport mode dynamic auto command configures the switch port to negotiate trunking with the connected port using Dynamic Trunking Protocol (DTP).

217. **Answer:** B) redistribute ospf

Explanation: The redistribute ospf command within EIGRP configuration mode is used to redistribute OSPF routes into EIGRP.

218. **Answer:** A) TACACS+ encrypts the entire payload, while RADIUS only encrypts the password.

Explanation: TACACS+ (Terminal Access Controller Access-Control System Plus) encrypts the entire payload of the access-request packet, whereas RADIUS (Remote Authentication Dial-In User Service) only encrypts the password in the access-request packet.

219. **Answer:** B) The time an OSPF router waits to declare a neighbor down.

Explanation: The ip ospf dead-interval command configures the time an OSPF router waits to declare a neighbor down after not receiving Hello packets.

220. **Answer:** C) Blocking

Explanation: STP/RSTP places interfaces not chosen to be in a forwarding state into a blocking state to prevent loops.

221. **Answer:** B) To prevent looping frames

Explanation: STP (Spanning Tree Protocol) and RSTP (Rapid Spanning Tree Protocol) primarily function to eliminate network loops by selectively blocking redundant paths in Ethernet networks. This ensures a loop-free topology, preventing broadcast storms and maintaining network stability.

222. **Answer:** C) All working interfaces

Explanation: On the root switch in a spanning tree topology, all interfaces are designated as forwarding state, allowing them to actively pass traffic without any blocking to maintain network connectivity and efficiency.

223. **Answer:** B) Designated switch

Explanation: In a spanning tree topology, the designated switch is determined based on the lowest accumulated path cost to the root bridge, ensuring efficient forwarding of frames within the network by minimizing delays and optimizing traffic paths.

224. **Answer:** C) Broadcast storms

Explanation: STP (Spanning Tree Protocol) and RSTP (Rapid Spanning Tree Protocol) are designed to eliminate redundant paths in Ethernet networks, preventing broadcast storms by ensuring a loop-free topology where only one active path exists between any two network devices at a time.

225. **Answer:** B) It only forwards STP/RSTP messages

Explanation: When a switch interface is in a blocking state, it only forwards STP/RSTP messages and does not send or receive user traffic.

226. **Answer:** B) When MAC address tables keep changing due to looping frames

Explanation: MAC table instability occurs when the switch's MAC address table keeps changing due to looping frames.

227. **Answer:** C) To maintain the STP/RSTP topology

Explanation: The Hello Bridge Protocol Data Unit (BPDU) is regularly exchanged between switches to verify connectivity and ensure consistent spanning tree topology. It helps switches identify the root bridge, calculate path costs, and determine the best path to prevent loops in the network.

VERSAtile Reads

228. **Answer:** B) Priority and MAC address

Explanation: The Bridge ID (BID) uniquely identifies each bridge in a spanning tree domain. It combines a configurable priority value, which determines the root bridge and designated ports, with the bridge's MAC address to create a hierarchical structure for loop prevention and network stability.

229. **Answer:** B) The switch with the lowest MAC address wins

Explanation: If a tie occurs in the root election based on priority, the switch with the lowest MAC address wins.

230 **Answer:** B) Every 2 seconds

Explanation: By default, the root switch sends Hello BPDUs at intervals of 2 seconds to announce its presence and maintain network topology information. These BPDUs help switches determine the root bridge and calculate the shortest path to it, ensuring efficient data forwarding and loop prevention in the network.

231. **Answer:** B) The port with the lowest cost

Explanation: The designated port (DP) is the port with the lowest cost on a LAN segment.

232. **Answer:** B) The port with the least cost to the root switch

Explanation: The root port (RP) on a non-root switch is the port with the least cost to the root switch.

233. **Answer:** B) To prevent loops and ensure all devices can communicate

Explanation: The main goal of STP/RSTP is to prevent loops and ensure all devices in a VLAN can communicate.

234. **Answer:** A) Electing a root switch

Explanation: The first step in the STP/RSTP process is to elect a root bridge among all the switches in the network. This root bridge serves as the central point from which all spanning tree calculations and decisions originate, ensuring a loop-free topology.

235. **Answer:** B) Lowest administrative cost to the root switch

Explanation: STP/RSTP chooses the root port based on the lowest administrative cost to the root switch.

236. **Answer:** B) The indefinite looping of broadcast frames in a network

Explanation: A broadcast storm is the indefinite looping of broadcast frames in a network.

237. **Answer:** A) To ensure all parts of the LAN are connected

Explanation: It is important for all devices in a VLAN to send frames to each other to ensure all parts of the LAN are connected.

238. **Answer:** B) The process of determining which ports to block and forward

Explanation: STP convergence refers to the process of determining which ports to block and forward.

239. **Answer:** B) By adding an additional check on each interface before using it to send/receive user traffic

Answers

VERSAtile Reads

Explanation: STP/RSTP prevents looping frames by adding an additional check on each interface before using it to send/receive user traffic.

240. **Answer:** B) The switch forwards frames to the wrong locations

Explanation: When a switch's MAC address table keeps changing due to looping frames, the switch forwards frames to the wrong locations.

241. **Answer:** B) The port that receives the least-cost Hello BPDU from the root switch

Explanation: The root port on a non-root switch is the port that receives the least-cost Hello BPDU from the root switch.

242. **Answer:** B) It significantly impacts end-user device performance

Explanation: A broadcast storm significantly impacts end-user device performance.

243. **Answer:** B) The port does not forward user frames or learn MAC addresses

Explanation: Blocking a port in STP/RSTP means the port does not forward user frames or learn MAC addresses.

244. **Answer:** B) When it has the lowest root cost

Explanation: A switch is considered the designated switch on a link when it has the lowest root cost.

245. **Answer:** B) It reacts and starts the process of changing the spanning-tree topology

Explanation: If a switch does not receive a Hello BPDU within the expected time, it reacts and starts the process of changing the spanning-tree topology.

246. Answer: B) To indicate the switch's cost to reach the root switch

 Explanation: The root cost field in the Hello BPDU indicates the switch's cost to reach the root switch.

247. Answer: C) All working interfaces

 Explanation: All working interfaces on a root switch are placed in a forwarding state.

248. Answer: B) It results in multiple copies of one frame being delivered to the host

 Explanation: Multiple frame transmission caused by looping frames results in multiple copies of one frame being delivered to the host.

249. Answer: B) To identify the switch that sent the Hello BPDU

 Explanation: The sender's bridge ID field in the Hello BPDU identifies the switch that sent the Hello BPDU.

250. Answer: B) To forward frames onto the LAN segment

 Explanation: The designated port (DP) forwards frames onto the LAN segment.

251. Answer: B) Based on the lowest root cost

 Explanation: STP/RSTP chooses the designated port on a LAN segment based on the lowest root cost.

252. Answer: B) To ensure all interfaces become designated ports (DPs)

Explanation: In a Spanning Tree Protocol (STP) topology, the root switch (or root bridge) is the central point of reference for all spanning tree calculations. The root switch places all of its working interfaces in a forwarding state to ensure that it can communicate with all other switches in the network. These interfaces become designated ports (DPs) on the root switch. The primary purpose is to facilitate the optimal and loop-free path of network traffic across the network.

253. **Answer:** B) To forward frames to the root switch

Explanation: The root port (RP) on a non-root switch is the port that has the best path (lowest cost) to the root switch. Its primary function is to forward frames towards the root switch.

254. **Answer:** B) It changes the Hello to list the forwarding switch's own BID and root cost

Explanation: When a switch forwards a Hello BPDU received from the root switch, it updates the Hello BPDU with its own Bridge ID (BID) and the accumulated cost to reach the root switch before sending it out on its designated ports.

255. **Answer:** B) It stops advertising itself as root and forwards the superior Hello

Explanation: When a switch receives a superior Hello BPDU (one indicating a better path to the root), it stops advertising itself as the root and begins forwarding the superior BPDU. This helps in recalculating the spanning tree.

256. **Answer:** B) Chooses the port with the lowest neighbor bridge ID

Explanation: If there is a tie in the root cost, STP/RSTP will choose the port with the lowest neighbor bridge ID (Bridge ID of the neighboring switch on the other end of the link).

257. **Answer:** B) It reacts and starts the process of changing the spanning-tree topology

Explanation: If a switch does not receive a Hello BPDU from the root switch within a certain time (Max Age timer), it assumes a topology change and initiates a process to re-elect a new root bridge and recalculate the spanning tree.

258. **Answer:** B) To indicate the switch's cost to reach the root switch

Explanation: The root cost field in the Hello BPDU indicates the cumulative cost to reach the root switch from the sending switch.

259. **Answer:** B) The port does not forward user frames or learn MAC addresses

Explanation: In STP/RSTP, a port in the blocking state does not forward user frames and does not learn MAC addresses. It only listens to BPDUs.

260. **Answer:** C) All working interfaces

Explanation: On the root switch, all working interfaces are placed in the forwarding state because they serve as designated ports (DPs) for their respective network segments.

261. **Answer:** B) To prevent looping frames

Explanation: The main purpose of STP (Spanning Tree Protocol) and RSTP (Rapid Spanning Tree Protocol) is to prevent frame looping by creating a loop-free logical topology in Ethernet networks.

262. **Answer:** A) To set the trunking mode to 802.1Q

Explanation: The switchport trunk encapsulation dot1q command configures the trunk port to use 802.1Q encapsulation, which is an industry standard for VLAN tagging.

263. **Answer:** B) EIGRP

Explanation: EIGRP (Enhanced Interior Gateway Routing Protocol) uses the multicast address 224.0.0.10 to send updates and queries to its neighbors.

264. **Answer:** C) EtherChannel

Explanation: EtherChannel is a Cisco technology that allows multiple physical links to be bundled together into a single logical link for increased bandwidth and redundancy.

265. **Answer:** B) To prevent rogue DHCP servers

Explanation: DHCP snooping is a security feature on switches that filters DHCP messages and ensures only trusted DHCP servers can assign IP addresses to clients. This prevents rogue DHCP servers from distributing unauthorized IP addresses.

266. **Answer:** B) Listening

Explanation: In the Listening state, a switch port can send and receive Bridge Protocol Data Units (BPDUs) but does not forward user data. This state is used to determine if the port should transition to the Forwarding or Blocking state.

267. **Answer:** C) ipv6 unicast-routing

Explanation: The ipv6 unicast-routing command is used to enable IPv6 routing on a Cisco router, allowing it to forward IPv6 packets.

268. Answer: C) It forwards DHCP requests to a specified DHCP server.

Explanation: The ip helper-address command is used to forward DHCP broadcast requests to a specified DHCP server. This is particularly useful in environments where the DHCP server is not on the same subnet as the client devices.

269. A) show ip eigrp neighbors

Explanation: The show ip eigrp neighbors command displays the list of EIGRP neighbors (adjacencies) and information about their state and status.

270. Answer: C) Larger subnets

Explanation: Having more host bits in a subnet mask results in larger subnets.

271. Answer: D) All of the above

Explanation: A subnet mask defines the network and host portions of an IP address and determines the size of a subnet.

272. Answer: D) Both B and C

Explanation: Using a single-size subnet simplifies operation but also increases IP address waste.

273. Answer: A) Variable-Length Subnet Mask

Explanation: VLSM (Variable-Length Subnet Mask) allows subnet masks of different lengths to be applied to different subnets within the same network address space, optimizing IP address allocation and subnet utilization. This flexibility is crucial in efficiently managing IP addresses in complex network environments.

274. Answer: D) Both B and C

 Explanation: Using VLSM in a network design increases the number of subnets and allows for more efficient use of IP addresses.

275. Answer: A) It determines the number of available IP addresses in the subnet

 Explanation: The right mask for each subnet determines the number of available IP addresses in the subnet.

276. Answer: B) The number of devices that need IP addresses

 Explanation: The primary consideration when determining the number of hosts per subnet is the number of devices that need IP addresses.

277. Answer: C) By counting the number of locations that need a subnet

 Explanation: The engineer determines the number of subnets required by counting the number of locations that need a subnet.

278. Answer: B) They must not be separated by any router

 Explanation: IP addresses in the same subnet must not be separated by any router.

279. Answer: A) They must be separated by at least one router

 Explanation: IP addresses in different subnets must be separated by at least one router.

280. Answer: B) To forward packets from one subnet to another

 Explanation: The main job of a router in a subnetted network is to forward packets from one subnet to another.

281. **Answer:** B) To filter network traffic

 Explanation: The primary purpose of an ACL is to filter network traffic by permitting or denying packets based on specified criteria.

282. **Answer:** B) It increases the number of available IP addresses

 Explanation: Using private IP networks in an enterprise internetwork increases the number of available IP addresses.

283. **Answer:** C) To identify the subnet within the network

 Explanation: The subnet number, also known as the subnet address, is a part of an IP address that identifies a specific subnet within a larger network. It's used in conjunction with the network address to distinguish between different subnets and route traffic accordingly.

284. **Answer:** B) The bits used to number different host IP addresses in the subnet

 Explanation: Host bits refer to the bits used to number different host IP addresses in the subnet.

285. **Answer:** B) It simplifies network configuration and operation

 Explanation: The advantage of using a single-size subnet is that it simplifies network configuration and operation.

286. **Answer:** B) It wastes IP addresses

 Explanation: Using a single-size subnet can lead to inefficient use of IP addresses because each subnet must be allocated a fixed number of IP addresses, regardless of the actual number of devices connected to it. This can result in unused or underutilized addresses within each subnet, leading to IP address wastage.

287. **Answer:** B) It allows for more efficient use of IP addresses

Explanation: The primary advantage of using VLSM is that it allows for more efficient use of IP addresses.

288. **Answer:** D) Both B and C

Explanation: Using different masks for different subnets in the same Class A network creates a more complex network design and allows for more efficient use of IP addresses.

289. **Answer:** B) To determine the number of required subnets and IP addresses per subnet

Explanation: The purpose of analyzing the addressing and subnetting needs of a network is to determine the number of required subnets and IP addresses per subnet.

290. **Answer:** B) Simplified network operation

Explanation: Using a single mask for all subnets in a network results in simplified network operation.

291. **Answer:** B) Analyze needs

Explanation: Analyzing needs is the first step to determine the number of subnets and hosts required.

292. **Answer:** C) Spreadsheet or subnet-planning tool

Explanation: Using a spreadsheet or subnet-planning tool helps in tracking subnets used in different locations.

293. Answer: D) UDP

Explanation: HSRP (Hot Standby Router Protocol) uses UDP port 1985 for communication between routers to provide redundancy for IP traffic. It allows a standby router to take over if the active router fails.

294. Answer: C) Route summarization

Explanation: Reserving ranges of subnets based on geographic locations simplifies route summarization.

295. Answer: C) .101 through .254

Explanation: The example shows DHCP pools assigned from .101 to .254 for LAN subnets.

296. Answer: A) Subnet locations, B) Static IP addresses, D) DHCP Ranges

Explanation: These are the key elements in planning the implementation of subnets.

297. Answer: D) Helps with route summarization

Explanation: A well-thought-out strategy for assigning subnets aids in route summarization.

298. Answer: C) Router

Explanation: Routers typically use static IP addresses for stability.

299. Answer: B) To communicate with all hosts in the network

Explanation: The network broadcast address is used to send packets to all hosts in the network.

300. **Answer:** B) 255.255.0.0

Explanation: The default subnet mask for a Class B network is indeed 255.255.0.0, which provides a range of IP addresses from 128.0.0.0 to 191.255.255.255. This allows for up to 65,534 hosts per subnet.

301. **Answer:** C) Multicast

Explanation: Class D addresses, designated within the range 224.0.0.0 to 239.255.255.255, are specifically reserved for multicast communication in IPv4 networks. These addresses are used to deliver packets simultaneously to multiple recipients, optimizing bandwidth usage for applications like multimedia streaming and online conferencing.

302. **Answer:** A) Class A

Explanation: Class A addresses, identified by their initial bit pattern of 0, are designated for large networks due to their structure that allows for a very large number of unique host addresses. The range spans from 0.0.0.0 to 127.255.255.255, with the first octet dedicated to network identification and the remaining three octets for host identification. This allocation provides flexibility and scalability, making it suitable for enterprises and organizations requiring extensive IP address space.

303. **Answer:** C) 16,777,214

Explanation: Class A networks indeed support a large number of hosts, specifically up to 16,777,214 hosts per network. The default subnet mask for a Class A network is 255.0.0.0, which provides a range of IP addresses from 0.0.0.0 to 127.255.255.255.

304. **Answer:** B) One address higher than the network ID

Explanation: In IPv4 addressing, the first usable address in a subnet is typically the one immediately following the network address. For example, if a network address is 192.168.1.0 with a subnet mask of 255.255.255.0 (/24), the first usable IP address would be 192.168.1.1. The network ID itself (192.168.1.0 in this case) is used to identify the network, while the subsequent addresses are available for assignment to hosts or devices on that network.

305. **Answer:** C) Class C network

Explanation: The subnet mask 255.255.255.0, also represented as /24 in CIDR notation, indicates a Class C network. Class C networks have a default subnet mask of 255.255.255.0 and are typically used for smaller networks that require fewer than 254 host addresses (since one address is reserved for the network address and one for the broadcast address).

306. **Answer:** C) 16,384

Explanation: Class B networks are identified by the range of IP addresses where the first octet ranges from 128 to 191 (binary starts with 10). The number of Class B networks can be calculated using $2^{14}=16,384$. This calculation derives from the fact that Class B networks use a 16-bit network portion of the IP address, leaving 14 bits for network addresses after the initial 2 bits (which are fixed as 10).

307. **Answer:** C) To dynamically lease IP addresses to hosts

Explanation: The primary purpose of the Dynamic Host Configuration Protocol (DHCP) is to dynamically lease IP addresses to hosts on a network. DHCP automates the process of assigning IP addresses, subnet masks, gateways, and other network configuration parameters, allowing devices to join the network with minimal manual configuration. This helps in efficient management and reuse of IP addresses within a network.

308. **Answer:** C) 192–223

Explanation: Class C networks range from 192 to 223 in the first octet of the IP address. This class designation is based on IP address ranges defined by the original IPv4 addressing scheme. Each class has a specific range of IP addresses allocated for network identification.

309. **Answer:** A) 254

 Explanation: Class C networks actually support up to 254 usable IP addresses for hosts. This is because in a Class C network, the first three octets (192.0.0.x to 223.255.255.x) are used for network identification, leaving 8 bits (or $2^8 - 2$) for host addresses after subnetting. The "-2" accounts for the network address and the broadcast address, which cannot be assigned to hosts. Therefore, a Class C network can have 254 usable hosts.

310. **Answer:** B) First two octets

 Explanation: In a Class B network address, the first two octets (16 bits) are dedicated to the network portion, while the remaining two octets (16 bits) are used for host addresses. This allows Class B networks to support a large number of hosts compared to Class A networks, but fewer than Class C networks.

311. **Answer:** A) 127.0.0.0

 Explanation: 127.0.0.0 is a reserved address range within the Class A network space, but it is not used for regular network communication. It is specifically reserved for loopback testing and is known as the loopback address. This address range allows a device to send network packets to itself, which is useful for testing network software without having to connect to a network.

312. **Answer:** C) Change the host octets to 255

 Explanation: That's correct. In IPv4 networking, the network broadcast address is determined by setting all host bits (in the host portion of the IP address) to 1, which corresponds to 255 in decimal.

313. Answer: C) 255.255.255.0

 Explanation: In IPv4 networking, the default subnet mask for a Class C network is 255.255.255.0. This subnet mask allows for up to 254 usable IP addresses within the network, with the first address reserved as the network address (typically ending in .0) and the last address reserved as the broadcast address (typically ending in .255). The remaining addresses (from .1 to .254) are available for hosts within that network.

314. Answer: D) Class D

 Explanation: Class D addresses, ranging from 224.0.0.0 to 239.255.255.255 in IPv4, are exclusively reserved for multicast communication. They allow efficient distribution of data to multiple hosts simultaneously, essential for applications like streaming, video conferencing, and online gaming.

315. Answer: B) 16

 Explanation: Class B addresses, identified by the range 128.0.0.0 to 191.255.255.255 in IPv4, allocate 16 bits for the network portion. This allows for a large number of networks, accommodating medium to large-sized organizations or internet service providers needing more than what Class A can provide.

316. Answer: B) Assign IP addresses

 Explanation: When assigning subnets to different locations, the second step is to assign IP addresses to the subnets. The first step typically involves identifying the locations or segments that need to be subnetted. Once the locations are identified, the appropriate subnets are created, and specific IP address ranges are assigned to each subnet. This step ensures that each subnet has a unique IP address range, facilitating organized and efficient network management. After assigning IP addresses, the subsequent steps would involve tracking the subnets used and configuring devices accordingly.

Answers

317. **Answer:** B) Location geography

 Explanation: Geography can influence the distribution of subnets for easier route summarization.

318. **Answer:** B) 4

 Explanation: With 2 bits, each bit can be either 0 or 1. The total number of unique combinations is calculated as $2^2=4$. These combinations are:

- 00
- 01
- 10
- 11

Each combination represents a unique binary sequence that can be used to represent different values or states in digital systems, such as in subnetting or encoding information.

319. **Answer:** A) OSPF

 Explanation: OSPF (Open Shortest Path First) is a link-state routing protocol that uses the Dijkstra algorithm to calculate the shortest path between nodes or routers in a network. The Dijkstra algorithm computes the shortest path tree from a single source node to all other nodes in the network based on the link costs. OSPF routers exchange link-state advertisements (LSAs) to build and maintain a topology database, from which they calculate the shortest paths using the Dijkstra algorithm.

320. **Answer:** B) 1.0.0.0–126.0.0.0

 Explanation: Class A networks encompass the IP address range from 1.0.0.0 to 126.255.255.255 in IPv4. This class provides the largest number of potential hosts per network, suitable for large-scale organizations or internet backbone networks requiring extensive address space.

321. **Answer:** B) 11111111 11111111 11111111 00001111

VERSAtile Reads

Explanation: The subnet mask should consist of contiguous 1s followed by contiguous 0s. Mixing 1s and 0s in an interleaved pattern is not valid according to subnetting rules in IPv4 addressing.

322. **Answer:** B) 255.255.255.240

Explanation: The binary 11110000 converts to decimal 240.

323. **Answer:** C) 18

Explanation: The prefix mask /18 indicates that the first 18 bits of the subnet mask are set to 1, defining the network portion of the IP address. This results in a subnet mask of 255.255.192.0 in decimal notation.

324. **Answer:** B) 11111111 11111111 11111111 00000000

Explanation: The prefix mask /24 signifies that the first 24 bits of the subnet mask are set to 1, defining the network portion of the IP address. This corresponds to a subnet mask of 255.255.255.0 in decimal notation, with the remaining 8 bits reserved for host addresses.

325. **Answer:** B) 18

Explanation: The subnet mask 255.255.192.0 is the same as a /18 CIDR notation. In binary, /18 indicates 18 bits are used for the network portion, allowing for 2^6 (64) subnets with 2^{14} (16,382) usable hosts per subnet.

326. **Answer:** C) /13

Explanation: Counting the 1s in the binary mask 11111111 11111000 00000000 00000000 confirms there are 13 ones, indicating a subnet mask with a /13 prefix length (2^{13} = 8192 possible subnets).

327. **Answer:** C) 255.255.252.0

Explanation: The binary mask 11111111 11111111 11111100 00000000 is converted to its decimal equivalent by evaluating each 8-bit segment separately. The first and second octets, 11111111, both convert to 255 because all bits are set to 1, which is 128+64+32+16+8+4+2+1128 + 64 + 32 + 16 + 8 + 4 + 2 + 1128+64+32+16+8+4+2+1. The third octet, 11111100, converts to 252, as the first six bits are set to 1, giving 128+64+32+16+8+4128 + 64 + 32 + 16 + 8 + 4128+64+32+16+8+4. The fourth octet, 00000000, converts to 0 since all bits are 0. Combining these, the decimal equivalent of the binary mask is 255.255.252.0

328. **Answer:** C) 255.255.255.224

Explanation: The prefix mask /27 has 27 binary 1s, which converts to 224 in the last octet.

329. **Answer:** A) /21

Explanation: The subnet mask 255.255.248.0, represented in binary as 11111111.11111111.11111000.00000000, contains 21 binary 1s in total. This mask corresponds to a subnet prefix length of /21 in CIDR notation, indicating that the first 21 bits are used for network identification.

330. **Answer:** D) 256

Explanation: A valid subnet mask octet, which represents part of an IPv4 address's subnet mask, must indeed range between 0 and 255 inclusive. This range corresponds to all possible values that an octet in an IPv4 address can hold, as each octet is represented by 8 bits, allowing for values from 0 (00000000 in binary) to 255 (11111111 in binary).

331. **Answer:** A) 11111111 11111111 11111111 11111100

Explanation: The binary equivalent of the subnet mask 255.255.255.252 is 11111111.11111111.11111111.11111100. This mask is used to subnet a network into smaller subnets, allowing for up to 4 subnets with 30 host addresses each.

332. Answer: A) 12

Explanation: The prefix mask /20 corresponds to a subnet mask of 255.255.240.0 in dotted decimal notation. This provides 12 bits for the host part of the IP address, allowing for up to 4094 usable host addresses per subnet.

333. Answer: C) /26

Explanation: The prefix mask /26 corresponds to a subnet mask of 255.255.255.192 in dotted decimal notation. This subnet mask has 26 binary 1s in its representation, leaving 6 bits for the host part of the IP address. This allows for a maximum of 62 usable host addresses per subnet.

334. Answer: B) 255.255.252.0

Explanation: The binary mask "11111100 00000000" converts to 252.0 in decimal notation. This represents the subnet mask 255.255.252.0, which is used to define a subnet with 10 bits for the network portion and 22 bits for the host portion in an IPv4 address.

335. Answer: A) 254

Explanation: The subnet mask 255.255.255.0, or /24, provides 254 usable IP addresses within a network, after subtracting the network address and the broadcast address.

336. Answer: B) 255.255.192.0

Explanation: The prefix mask /18 corresponds to 255.255.192.0.

337. Answer: C) /28

Explanation: The subnet mask 255.255.255.240 is a 28-bit mask in CIDR notation. To determine the CIDR notation (prefix mask), count the number of continuous 1s in the subnet mask:

255.255.255.240 in binary is 11111111.11111111.11111111.11110000.

Counting the continuous 1s gives us 28 bits. Therefore, the corresponding CIDR notation is /28.

338. **Answer:** D) Star network

Explanation: In a star network topology, all devices (nodes) are connected to a central hub or switch, facilitating centralized management and easy scalability.

339. **Answer:** B) Redundant paths between nodes

Explanation: A full mesh network topology provides redundant paths between every pair of nodes, which enhances fault tolerance and ensures multiple communication paths.

340. **Answer:** B) 255.255.248.0

Explanation: The binary mask 11111000 00000000 converts to the decimal subnet mask 248.0 in IPv4 notation. This represents a subnet mask where the first 5 bits are used for the network portion and the remaining 27 bits are used for host addresses within that network.

341. **Answer:** B) /30

Explanation: The subnet mask 255.255.255.252 corresponds to the prefix mask /30 in IPv4. This means there are 30 bits allocated for the network portion and 2 bits for host addresses, resulting in a subnet that can accommodate up to 2 usable hosts (after excluding the network and broadcast addresses).

342. **Answer:** A) 255.255.0.0

 Explanation: The prefix mask /16 corresponds to the subnet mask 255.255.0.0 in IPv4 notation. This subnet mask indicates that the first 16 bits of the IP address are used for network identification, and the remaining 16 bits are used for host identification within that network.

343. **Answer:** B) 25

 Explanation: The subnet mask 255.255.255.128, in binary representation, has 25 consecutive binary 1s. This corresponds to the first 3 octets (255.255.255) being fully masked (all bits set to 1) and the last octet (128) having its highest bit set to 1, with the remaining bits set to 0. This configuration effectively creates a subnet with 25 bits dedicated to the network portion of the IP address.

344. **Answer:** B) 11111111 11111111 11111100 00000000

 Explanation: The prefix mask /22 in CIDR (Classless Inter-Domain Routing) notation specifies a subnet mask where the first 22 bits are set to 1, indicating the network portion of the IP address. In binary, this translates to 11111111.11111111.11111100.00000000. The remaining 10 bits are set to 0, representing the host portion. This subnet mask allows for the creation of multiple subnets within a larger network, each with its own unique range of IP addresses. Subnetting with a /22 prefix mask provides a balance between efficient use of IP addresses and manageable network size, accommodating up to 1024 (2^{10}) hosts per subnet.

345. **Answer:** A) 2

 Explanation: A /30 subnet mask allocates 30 bits for network identification, leaving 2 bits for host addresses. This configuration allows for a total of 4 IP addresses per subnet, with 2 addresses usable for devices. It's typically used in scenarios like point-to-point links where only two devices need direct communication.

346. Answer: B) 255.255.255.254

Explanation: The prefix mask /31 corresponds to the subnet mask 255.255.255.254 in IPv4 notation. It signifies a network with 31 bits allocated for the network portion and 1 bit for host addresses, suitable for point-to-point links.

347. Answer: B) /25

Explanation: The subnet mask 255.255.255.128, when converted to CIDR notation, corresponds to the prefix mask /25. This means it provides 25 bits for the network portion of the IP address, allowing for $2^{(32-25)}$ = 128 IP addresses in each subnet.

348. Answer: A) 11111111 11111111 11111110 00000000

Explanation: The binary representation 11111110 00000000 corresponds to the subnet mask 255.255.254.0 in IPv4, indicating 23 bits for the network portion and 9 bits for the host portion, allowing for larger subnet sizes within the same class network range.

349. Answer: B) 255.255.255.254

Explanation: The binary mask 11111111 11111111 11111111 11111110 converts to the decimal subnet mask 255.255.255.254 in IPv4, which designates 31 bits for the network portion and 1 bit for host addressing, typically used in point-to-point links where only two addresses are needed.

350. Answer: B) 12

Explanation: The subnet mask 255.255.252.0 in binary is represented as 11111111.11111111.11111100.00000000. A subnet mask is 32 bits long, and the number of binary 0s in this subnet mask is the count of the 0s in the binary representation. In this case, there are 10 binary 0s in the last octet and 2 binary 0s in the third octet, making a total of 12 binary 0s.

351. **Answer:** C) ping

Explanation: The ping command can be used with both IPv4 and IPv6 addresses. On Cisco devices, simply using ping followed by the IPv6 address will initiate an IPv6 ping.

352. **Answer:** B) It is a backup route stored in the topology table.

Explanation: A feasible successor in EIGRP is a backup route that satisfies the feasibility condition and is stored in the topology table. It can be used immediately if the primary route (successor) fails.

353. **Answer:** B) The default gateway must reside within the same VLAN as the hosts.

Explanation: The default gateway must be on the same VLAN as the hosts to provide a point of exit for traffic destined for other networks. It typically has an IP address within the same subnet as the hosts.

354. **Answer:** B) It uniquely identifies the OSPF process on the router.

Explanation: The router-id command in OSPF configuration is used to assign a unique identifier to the OSPF process on the router, which is used to distinguish it from other routers in the OSPF domain.

355. **Answer:** A) ipv6 address

Explanation: The ipv6 address command is used to assign an IPv6 address to an interface on a Cisco router.

356. **Answer:** A) NDP

Explanation: Neighbor Discovery Protocol (NDP) is used in IPv6 networks to perform functions similar to ARP in IPv4, such as discovering other network nodes and their link-layer addresses.

357. **Answer:** C) To prevent network loops.

Explanation: The primary purpose of Spanning Tree Protocol (STP) is to prevent network loops in a Layer 2 network by creating a loop-free logical topology.

358. **Answer:** A) access-list 100 permit tcp host 192.168.1.1 eq 80

Explanation: The command access-list 100 permit tcp host 192.168.1.1 eq 80 creates an access control list that permits HTTP traffic (TCP port 80) from the specified host (192.168.1.1).

359. **Answer:** A) To disable DNS lookup when a command is mistyped.

Explanation: The no ip domain-lookup command is used to disable the DNS lookup feature on a Cisco router, which prevents the router from attempting to resolve mistyped commands as hostnames.

360. **Answer:** A) 224.0.0.5

Explanation: OSPF uses the multicast address 224.0.0.5 to communicate with all OSPF routers on the local network segment. This address is used for sending OSPF Hello packets and Link State Advertisements (LSAs).

361. **Answer:** A) bandwidth

Explanation: The bandwidth command is used in interface configuration mode to set the bandwidth of a serial interface. This value is used by routing protocols to calculate the metric.

362. **Answer:** A) To configure a Service Level Agreement (SLA) monitoring operation.

Explanation: The ip sla command is used to configure SLA monitoring operations on Cisco devices, which can be used to measure network performance.

363. **Answer:** A) show ip nat translations

Explanation: The show ip nat translations command displays the current NAT translations, showing the mappings between inside local and inside global addresses.

364. **Answer:** B) 10 seconds

Explanation: The default hold time for EIGRP hello packets is 10 seconds. If a router does not receive a hello packet from a neighbor within this time, it considers the neighbor down.

365. **Answer:** C) RIP

Explanation: RIP version 2 uses the multicast address 224.0.0.9 to send routing updates to other RIP-enabled routers on the local network.

366. **Answer:** A) To provide redundancy for default gateways

Explanation: HSRP (Hot Standby Router Protocol) provides redundancy for default gateways by allowing multiple routers to participate in a virtual router group, with one router acting as the active router and another as the standby.

367. **Answer:** A) ip route

Explanation: The ip route command is used to configure a static route in a Cisco router, specifying the destination network, subnet mask, and next-hop address or exit interface.

368. Answer: B) Data Link layer

Explanation: The MAC (Media Access Control) address operates at the Data Link layer (Layer 2) of the OSI model and is used for addressing within a local network segment.

369. Answer: A) show ip route

Explanation: The show ip route command displays the IP routing table on a Cisco router, listing all known routes and their respective next hops and metrics.

370. Answer: A) PAP and CHAP

Explanation: PPP (Point-to-Point Protocol) uses PAP (Password Authentication Protocol) and CHAP (Challenge Handshake Authentication Protocol) for authentication between two peer devices.

371. Answer: C) ipv6 unicast-routing

Explanation: The ipv6 unicast-routing command is used to enable IPv6 routing on a Cisco router, allowing the router to forward IPv6 packets.

372. Answer: B) To enable the interface

Explanation: The no shutdown command is used to enable an interface on a Cisco router or switch that has been administratively shut down.

373. Answer: A) ip dhcp pool

Explanation: The ip dhcp pool command is used to define a DHCP pool on a Cisco router, which includes specifying the IP address range and other DHCP options for the pool.

374. Answer: B) To translate private IP addresses to public IP addresses

Explanation: The primary function of Network Address Translation (NAT) is to translate private IP addresses used within a local network to public IP addresses for communication over the Internet.

375. **Answer:** A) show interfaces

Explanation: The show interfaces command displays detailed information about the status and configuration of a specific interface or all interfaces on a Cisco router.

376. **Answer:** B) Power over Ethernet

Explanation: PoE stands for Power over Ethernet, which is a technology that allows Ethernet cables to carry electrical power to devices such as IP phones, wireless access points, and cameras.

377. **Answer:** A) ip routing

Explanation: The ip routing command enables IPv4 packet forwarding on a Cisco router, allowing the router to forward packets between different network interfaces.

378. **Answer:** A) ip access-group

Explanation: The ip access-group command is used to apply an access control list (ACL) to an interface on a Cisco router, specifying whether to use the ACL for inbound or outbound traffic.

379. **Answer:** A) VLAN 1

Explanation: By default, all ports on a Cisco switch are assigned to VLAN 1, which is the default VLAN used for management and initial configuration.

380. **Answer:** C) BGP

Explanation: BGP (Border Gateway Protocol) uses TCP port 179 for establishing connections and exchanging routing information between BGP peers.

381. **Answer:** B) Totally Stubby Area

Explanation: A Totally Stubby Area in OSPF is a type of area that does not accept summary LSAs (Type 3) from other areas, except for the default route (0.0.0.0). This reduces the size of the routing table and simplifies the routing process within the area.

382. **Answer:** B) 110

Explanation: The default administrative distance for OSPF (Open Shortest Path First) routes is 110. This distance is used to determine the trustworthiness of the route learned via OSPF compared to routes learned via other protocols.

383. **Answer:** A) redistribute ospf 1 metric 1000

Explanation: The redistribute ospf 1 metric 1000 command is used under the EIGRP configuration mode to redistribute OSPF routes into EIGRP with a specified metric of 1000.

384. **Answer:** C) Unique Local

Explanation: Unique Local IPv6 addresses (ULA) are similar to private IPv4 addresses. They are intended for local communication within a site or organization and are not routable on the global Internet.

385. **Answer:** A) channel-group 1 mode active

Explanation: The channel-group 1 mode active command is used in interface configuration mode to add the interface to an EtherChannel using the Link Aggregation Control Protocol (LACP) in active mode.

386. Answer: A) To set the next hop for iBGP routes to the IP address of the local router

Explanation: The next-hop-self command in BGP is used to modify the next hop attribute of iBGP-learned routes to the IP address of the local router, ensuring that internal peers use the local router as the next hop.

387. Answer: A) NTP

Explanation: Network Time Protocol (NTP) is used to synchronize the clocks of network devices to a common time source, ensuring accurate timekeeping across the network.

388. Answer: D) Stateless address autoconfiguration (SLAAC)

Explanation: One of the main advantages of IPv6 is Stateless Address Autoconfiguration (SLAAC), which allows devices to automatically configure their own IP addresses without the need for a DHCP server.

389. Answer: C) show ip ospf neighbor

Explanation: The show ip ospf neighbor command displays the current OSPF neighbor relationships, including the state of each neighbor and the interface on which the OSPF packets are being exchanged.

390. Answer: B) Trunking

Explanation: Trunking allows multiple VLANs to be configured on a single switchport, enabling the port to carry traffic for multiple VLANs between switches or other network devices.

391. Answer: B) logging host

Explanation: The logging host command is used to configure a router to send all log messages to a specified syslog server. This helps in centralizing log management.

392. **Answer:** A) To set the maximum segment size for TCP packets

Explanation: The ip tcp adjust-mss command is used to set the Maximum Segment Size (MSS) for TCP packets, which can help prevent fragmentation in the network.

393. **Answer:** B) EIGRP

Explanation: EIGRP (Enhanced Interior Gateway Routing Protocol) uses the Diffusing Update Algorithm (DUAL) to calculate loop-free and efficient routes, ensuring quick convergence and reliability.

394. **Answer:** B) show ip ospf database

Explanation: The show ip ospf database command provides detailed information about the OSPF Link State Advertisements (LSAs) stored in the OSPF database.

395. **Answer:** A) area range

Explanation: The area range command is used in OSPF to summarize routes at an area border router (ABR). This helps reduce the size of the routing table and minimize routing updates.

396. **Answer:** A) VLANs

Explanation: VLANs (Virtual Local Area Networks) allow a network to be segmented into multiple broadcast domains using a single physical switch, providing isolation and improved network performance.

397. Answer: A) Reduced size of the routing table

Explanation: Route summarization in OSPF helps reduce the size of the routing table by aggregating multiple specific routes into a single summary route. This improves efficiency and scalability.

398. Answer: A) Virtual IP

Explanation: HSRP (Hot Standby Router Protocol) uses a Virtual IP address that is shared among a group of routers, ensuring that one IP address is used for the virtual router, providing gateway redundancy.

399. Answer: A) router bgp <AS-number>

Explanation: The router bgp <AS-number> command is used to enable BGP on a router and specify the local Autonomous System (AS) number.

400. Answer: A) show spanning-tree vlan <vlan-id>

Explanation: The show spanning-tree vlan <vlan-id> command displays the current spanning-tree configuration for a specific VLAN on a Cisco switch, including information about the root bridge, port states, and costs.

About Our Products

Other products from VERSAtile Reads are:

 Elevate Your Leadership: The 10 Must-Have Skills

 Elevate Your Leadership: 8 Effective Communication Skills

 Elevate Your Leadership: 10 Leadership Styles for Every Situation

 300+ PMP Practice Questions Aligned with PMBOK 7, Agile Methods, and Key Process Groups – 2024

 Exam-Cram Essentials Last-Minute Guide to Ace the PMP Exam - Your Express Guide featuring PMBOK® Guide

 Career Mastery Blueprint - Strategies for Success in Work and Business

 Memory Magic: Unraveling the Secret of Mind Mastery

 The Success Equation Psychological Foundations For Accomplishment

 Fairy Dust Chronicles – The Short and Sweet of Wonder

 B2B Breakthrough – Proven Strategies from Real-World Case Studies

About Our Products

 CISSP Fast Track Master: CISSP Essentials for Exam Success

 CISA Fast Track Master: CISA Essentials for Exam Success

 CISM Fast Track Master: CISM Essentials for Exam Success

 CCSP Fast Track Master: CCSP Essentials for Exam Success

 CLF-C02: AWS Certified Cloud Practitioner: Fast Track to Exam Success

 ITIL 4 Foundation Essentials: Fast Track to Exam Success

 CCNP Security Essentials: Fast Track to Exam Success

 Certified SCRUM Master Exam Cram Essentials

 Six Sigma Green Belt Exam Cram: Essentials for Exam Success

 Microsoft 365 Fundamentals: Fast Track to Exam Success

www.ingramcontent.com/pod-product-compliance
Lightning Source LLC
LaVergne TN
LVHW081344050326
832903LV00024B/1313